Banwell Hill: A Lay of the Seven Seas by William Lisle Bowles

William Lisle Bowles was born on 24th September 1762 at King's Sutton in Northamptonshire.

His great-grandfather, grandfather and his father, William Thomas Bowles, had all been parish priests and inevitably Bowles would join their line.

In 1789 Bowles published, a small quarto volume, Fourteen Sonnets, which was received with extraordinary praise, not only by the general public, but by such revered poets as Samuel Taylor Coleridge and Wordsworth.

After receiving his degree at Oxford, Bowles now began his career in service to the Church of England.

His years of service perhaps diminished both his stature as a poet and certainly the way he was viewed. For much of his career Bowles was seen as rather soft when set against his contemporaries but in the end his ability as a poet was enshrined, after a long and ferocious attack against him, by the principles he so eloquently wrote about and adhered too.

In personality and nature Bowles was said to be an amiable, absent-minded, but rather eccentric man. His poems speak warmly of a refinement of feeling, tenderness, and pensive thought, but are lacking in power and passion. But that should not diminish their value or appreciation to us.

Bowles maintained that images drawn from nature are poetically finer than those drawn from art; and that in the highest kinds of poetry the themes or passions handled should be of the general or elemental kind, and not the transient manners of any society.

As well as his poetry Bowles was also responsible for writing a Life of Bishop Ken (in two volumes, 1830–1831), Coombe Ellen and St. Michael's Mount (1798), The Battle of the Nile (1799), and The Sorrows of Switzerland (1801).

William Lisle Bowles died on April 7th, 1850 at the age of 87.

Index of Contents

PREFACE

The estimation of a Poem of this nature must depend, first, on its arrangement, plan, and disposition; secondly, on the judgment, propriety, and feeling with which—in just and proper succession and relief— picture, pathos, moral and religious reflections, historical notices, or affecting incidents, are interwoven. Thereader will, in the next place, attend to the versification, or music, in which the thoughts are conveyed. Shakspeare and Milton are the great masters of the verse I have adopted. But who can be heard after them? The reader, however, will at least find no specimens of sonorous harmony ending with such significant words as "of," "and," "if," "but," etc of which we have had lately some splendid examples. I would therefore only request of him to observe, that when such passages occur in this poem as "vanishing," "hush!" etc. it was from design, and not from want of ear.

An intermixture of images and characters from common life might be thought, at first sight, out of keeping with the higher tone of general colouring; but the interspersion of the comic, provided the due mock-heroic stateliness be kept up in the language, has often the effect of light and shade, as will be apparent on looking at Cowper's exquisite "Task," although he has often "offended against taste." The only difficulty is happily to steer "from grave to gay."

So far respecting the plan, the execution, the versification, and style. As to the sentiments conveyed in this poem, and in the notes, I must explicitly declare, that when I am convinced, as a clergyman and a magistrate, that there has been an increase of crime, owing, among other causes, to the system pursued by some "nominal Christians," who will not preach "these three" (faith, hope, and charity) according to the order of St Paul, but keep two of these graces, and the greatest of all, out of sight, upon any human plea or pretension; when they do not preach, "Add to your faith virtue;" when they will not preach, Christ died for the sins of "the world, and not for ours only;" when, from any pleas of their own, or persuaded by any sophistry or faction, they become, most emphatically, "dumb dogs" to the sublime and affecting moral parts of that gospel which they have engaged before God to deliver; and above all, when crimes, as I am verily persuaded have been, are, and must be, the consequence of such public preaching,—leaving others to "stand or fall" to their own God; I shall be guided by my own understanding, and the plain Word of God, as I find it earnestly, simply, beautifully, and divinely set before me by Christ and his Apostles; and so feeling, I shall as fearlessly deliver my own opinions, being assured, whether popular or unpopular, whether they offend this man or that, this sect or that sect, they will not easily be shaken.

I might ask, why did St Paul add, so emphatically, "these three," when he enumerated the Christian graces? Doubtless, because he thought the distinction very important. Why did St Peter say, "Add to your faith virtue"? Because he thought it equally important and essential. Why did St John say, "Christ died for the sins of the whole world, and not for ours only"? Because he thought it equally important and necessary.

Never omitting the atonement, justification by faith, the fruits of the Spirit, and never separating faith from its hallowed fellowship, we shall find all other parts of the gospel unite in harmonious subordination; but if we shade the moral parts down, leave them out, contradict them, by insidious sophistry, the Scripture, so far from being "rightly divided," will be discordant and clashing. The man, be he whom he may, who preaches "faith" without charity; who preaches "faith without virtue," is as pernicious and false an expounder of the divine message, as he who preaches "good works," without their legitimate and only foundation—Christian faith.

One would suppose, from the language of some preachers, the "civil," "decent," "moral" people, from the times of Baxter to the present, want amendment most. We all know that mere morals, which have no Christian basis, are not the gospel of Christ; but I might tell Richard, with great respect notwithstanding, for I respect his sincerity and his heart, that, at least, "decent," and "civil," and "moral" people, are not worse than indecent, immoral, and uncivil people; and when there are so many of these last, I think a word or two of reproof would not much hurt them, let the "decent," "moral," and "civil" be as wicked as they may.

I hope it is not necessary for me to disclaim, in speaking of facts, the most remote idea of throwing a slight on the sincerely pious of any portion of the community; but, if religion does not invigorate the higher feelings and principles of moral obligation; if a heartless and hollow jargon is often substituted for the fundamental laws of Christian obedience; if ostentatious affectation supersedes the meek, unobtrusive character of feminine devotion; if a petty peculiarity of system, a kind of conventional code of godliness, usurps the place of the specific righteousness, visible in its fruits, "of whatsoever things are honest, whatsoever things are just, whatsoever things are lovely;" if, to be fluent and flippant in the jargon of this petty peculiarity of code, is made the criterion of exclusive godliness; when, by thousands and thousands, after the example of Hawker, and others of the same school, Christianity is represented as having neither "an if, or but," the conclusion being left for the innumerable disciples of such a gospel school; when, because none—"no, not one"—is without sin, and none can stand upright in the sight of Him whose eyes are too pure to behold iniquity, they who have exercised themselves to "have a conscience void of offence toward God and man," though sensible of innumerable offences, are considered, by implication, before God, as no better than Burkes or Thurtles, for the imputation of utter depravity must mean this, or be mere hollow verba et voces; when amusements, or recreations, vicious only in their excess, are proclaimed as national abominations, while real abominations stalk abroad, as is the case in large manufacturing towns, with "the Lord," "the Lord," on the lips of some of the most depraved; when, from these causes, I do sincerely believe the heart has been hardened, and the understanding deteriorated, the wide effects being visible on the great criminal body of the nation,—I conceive I do a service to Evangelical Religion by speaking as I feel of that ludicrous caricature which so often in society usurps its name, and apes and disgraces its divine character.

I am not among those who divide the clergy of the Church of England into classes; and I think it my duty ingenuously to declare, that the opinions I have expressed of the effects of such public doctrines as I have described, be they preached or published by whom they may, were written without communication with any one living. I think it right to declare this, most explicitly, lest the distinguished person to whom this poem is inscribed, might be supposed to have any participation in such sentiments; though, I trust, no possible objection could be made to the manly avowal of my opinion of the injurious effects of Antinomian, or shades of Antinomian doctrines.

Further, the object of my remarks is not piety, but ostentatious publicity and affectation,—far more disgusting in the assumed garb of female piety than under any shape; and often attended by acting far more disgusting than any acting on any stage.

BANWELL CAVE

The following extract of a letter from Mr Warner will enable the reader to form his own opinion concerning the vast accumulation of bones in this cave:—

"The sagacity of Mr Beard having detected the existence of the cavern, and his perseverance effected a precipitous descent into it, the objects offered to his notice were of the most astonishing and paradoxical description—'an antre vast,' rude from the hand of nature, of various elevations, and branching into several recesses; its floor overspread with a huge mingled mass of bones and mud, black earth (or decomposed animal matter), and sand from the Severn sea, which flows about six miles to the northward of Banwell village. The quantity of bones, and the mode by which they could be conveyed to, and deposited in, the place they occupied, were points of equal difficulty to be explained: as the former amounted to several waggon loads; and as no access to the cavern appeared to exist, except a fissure from above, utterly incapable, from its narrow dimensions, of admitting the falling in of any animal larger than a common sheep; whereas it was evident that huge quadrupeds, such as unknown beasts of the ox tribe, bears, wolves, and probably hyenas and tigers, had perished in the cave. But, though the questions how and when were unanswerable, this conclusion was irresistibly forced upon the mind, by the phenomena submitted to the eye, that, as the receptacle was infinitely too small to contain such a crowd of animals in their living state, they must necessarily have occupied it in succession: one portion of them after another paying the debt of nature, and (leaving their bones only, as a memorial of their existence on the spot) thus making room in the cavern for a succeeding set of inhabitants, of similarly ferocious habits to themselves. The difficulty, indeed, of the ingress of such beasts into the cave did not long continue to be invincible; as Mr Beard discovered and cleared out a lateral aperture in it, sufficiently inclining from the perpendicular, and sufficiently large in its dimensions, to admit of the easy descent into this subterraneous apartment of one of its unwieldy tenants, though loaded with its prey.

"From the circumstances premised, you will probably anticipate my thoughts on these remarkable phenomena; if not, they are as follow:—I consider the cavern to have been formed at the period of the original deposition and consolidation of the matter constituting the mountain limestone in which it is found; possibly by the agency of some elastic gas, imprisoned in the mass, which prevented the approximation of its particles to each other; or by some unaccountable interruption to the operation of the usual laws of its crystallization;—that, for a long succession of ages anterior to the Deluge, and previously to man's inhabiting the colder regions of the earth, Banwell Cave had been inhabited by successive generations of beasts of prey; which, as hunger dictated, issued from their den, pursued and slaughtered the gregarious animals, or wilder quadrupeds, in its neighbourhood; and dragged them, either bodily or piecemeal, to this retreat, in order to feast upon them at leisure, and undisturbed;—that the bottom of the cavern thus became a kind of charnel-house, of various and unnumbered beasts;— that this scene of excursive carnage continued till 'the flood came,' blending 'the oppressor with the oppressed,' and mixing the hideous furniture of the den with a quantity of extraneous matter, brought from the adjoining shore, and subjacent lands, by the waters of the Deluge, which rolled, surging (as Kirwan imagines), from the north-western quarter;—that, previously to this total submersion, as the flood increased on the lower grounds, the animals which fed upon them ascended the heights of Mendip, to escape impending death; and with panic rushed (as many as could gain entrance) into this dwelling-place of their worst enemies;—that numberless birds also, terrified by the elemental tumult, flew into the same den, as a place of temporary refuge;—that the interior of the cavern was speedily filled by the roaring Deluge, whose waters, dashing and crushing the various substances which they embraced, against the rugged rocks, or against each other; and continuing this violent and incessant action for at least three months, at length tore asunder every connected form, separated every skeleton, and produced that confusion of substances, that scene of disjecta membra, that mixture and disjunction of bones, which were apparent on the first inspection of the cavern; and which are now visible in that part of it which has been hitherto untouched."

Respecting the language of the Poem, I had nearly forgotten one remark. In almost all the local poems I have read, there is a confusion of the following nature. A local descriptive poem must consist, first, of the graphic view of the scenery around the spot from whence the view is taken; and, secondly, of the reflections and feelings which that view may be supposed to excite. The feelings of the heart naturally associate themselves with the idea of the tones of the supposed poetical harp; but external scenes are the province of the pencil, for the harp cannot paint woods and hills, and therefore, in almost all descriptive poems, the pencil and the lyre clash. Hence, in one page, the poet speaks of his lyre, and in the next, when he leaves feelings to paint to the eye, before the harp is out of the hand, he turns to the pencil! This fault is almost inevitable; the reader, therefore, will see in the first page of this Poem, that the graphic pencil is assumed, when the tones of the harp were inappropriate.

FOOTNOTES

Footnote : This poem, published in , was dedicated to Dr Henry Law, the Bishop of Bath and Wells.

Footnote : Of blank verse of the kind to which I have alluded, I am tempted to give a specimen:—

"'Twas summer, and we sailed to Greenwich in
A four-oared boat. The sun was shining, and
The scenes delightful; while we gazed on
The river winding, till we landed at
The Ship."

Footnote : Baxter's "Saints' Rest."

ARGUMENT

PART FIRST
Introduction—Retrospect—General view—Cave—Bones—Brief sketch of events since the deposit—Egypt—Druid—Roman—Saxon—Dane—Norman— Hill—Campanula—Bleadon—Weston—Steep Holms—Solitary flower on Steep Holms, the Peony—Flat Holms—Three unknown graves—Sea—Sea treacherous in its tranquillity—Mr Elton's children—Packet-boat sunk.

PART SECOND
First sound of the sea—First sight of the sea—Mother—Children—Uphill parsonage—Father—Wells clock—Clock figure—Contrast of village manners—Village maid—Rural nymph before the justices—State of agricultural districts—Cause of crime—Workhouse girl—Manufactory ranters—Prosing parson—Prig parson—Calvinistic commentators, etc.—Anti-moral preaching—True and false piety—Crimes passed over by anti-moral preachers—Bible, without note or comment—English Juggernaut—Village picture of Coombe—Village-school children, educated by Mrs P. Scrope—Annual meeting on the lawn of children—Old nurse—Benevolence of English landlords—Poor widow and daughter—Stourhead—Ken at Longleat—Marston house—Early travels in Switzerland—Compton house—Clergyman's wife—Village clergyman.

PART THIRD

A tale of a Cornish maid—Her prayer-book—Her mother—Widow and son—Tales of sea life—Phantom-ship of the Cape.

PART FOURTH

Solitary sea—Ship—Sea scenes of Southampton contrasted—Solitary sand—Young Lady—Severn—Walton Castle—Picture of Bristol—Congresbury—Brockley-Coombe—Fayland—Cottage—Poor Dinah—Goblin-Coombe—Langford court—Mendip lodge—Wrington—Blagdon—Author of the tune of "Auld Robin Gray"—Auld Robin Gray—Auld Lang Syne.

PART FIFTH

Lang syne—Return to the Deluge—Vision of the Flood—Archangel—Trump—Voice—Phantom-horse—Dove of the Ark—Dove ascending—Conclusion.

BANWELL HILL

PART FIRST

INTRODUCTION—GENERAL VIEW—CAVE—ASCENT—VIEW—STEEP HOLMS—FLAT HOLMS—SEA

If, gazing from this eminence, I wake,
With thronging thoughts, the harp of poesy
Once more, ere night descend, haply with tones
Fainter, and haply with a long farewell;
If, looking back upon the lengthened way
My feet have trod, since, long ago, I left
Those well-known shores, and when mine eyes are filled
With tears, I take the pencil in its turn,
And shading light the landscape spread below,
So smilingly beguile those starting tears;
Something, the feelings of the human heart—
Something, the scene itself, and something more—
A wish to gratify one generous mind—
May plead for pardon.
To this spot I came
To view the dark memorials of a world
Perished at the Almighty's voice, and swept
With all its noise away! Since then, unmarked,
In that rude cave those dark memorials lay,
And told no tale!
Spirit of other times,
Sad shadow of the ancient world, come forth!
Thou who has slept four thousand years, awake!
Rise from the cavern's last recess, and say,
What giant cleft in twain the neighbouring rocks,

Then slept for ages in vast Ogo's Cave,
And left them rent and frowning from that hour;
Say, rather, when the stern Archangel stood,
Above the tossing of the flood, what arm
Shattered this mountain, and its hollow chasm
Heaped with the mute memorials of that doom!
Spirit of other times, thou speakest not!
Yet who could gaze a moment on that wreck
Of desolation, but must pause to think
Of the mutations of the globe—of time,
Hurrying to onward spoil—of his own life,
Swift passing, as the summer light, away—
Of Him who spoke, and the dread storm went forth.
The surge came, and the surge went back, and there—
There—when the black abyss had ceased to roar,
And waters, shrinking from the rocks and hills,
Slept in the solitary sunshine—there
The bones that strew the inmost cavern lay:
And when forgotten centuries had passed,
And the gray smoke went up from villages,
And cities, with their towers and temples, shone,
And kingdoms rose and perished—there they lay!
The crow sailed o'er the spot; the villager
Plodded to morning toil, yet undisturbed
They lay:—when, lo! as if but yesterday
The Archangel's trump had thundered o'er the deep
The mighty shade of ages that are passed
Towers into light! Say, Christian, is it true,
That dim recess, that cavern, heaped with bones,
Will echo to thy Bible!
But a while
Here let me stand, and gaze upon the scene;
That headland, and those winding sands, and mark
The morning sunshine, on that very shore
Where once a child I wandered. Oh! return,
(I sigh) return a moment, days of youth,
Of childhood,—oh, return! How vain the thought,
Vain as unmanly! yet the pensive Muse,
Unblamed, may dally with imaginings;
For this wide view is like the scene of life,
Once traversed o'er with carelessness and glee,
And we look back upon the vale of years,
And hear remembered voices, and behold,
In blended colours, images and shades
Long passed, now rising, as at Memory's call,
Again in softer light.
I see thee not,
Home of my infancy—I see thee not,

Thou fane that standest on the hill alone,
The homeward sailor's sea-mark; but I view
Brean Down beyond; and there thy winding sands,
Weston; and, far away, one wandering ship,
Where stretches into mist the Severn sea.
There, mingled with the clouds, old Cambria draws
Its stealing line of mountains, lost in haze;
There, in mid-channel, sit the sister holms,
Secure and tranquil, though the tide's vast sweep,
As it rides by, might almost seem to rive
The deep foundations of the earth again,
Threatening, as once, resistless, to ascend
In tempest to this height, to bury here
Fresh-weltering carcases!
But, lo, the Cave!
Descend the steps, cut rudely in the rock,
Cautious. The yawning vault is at our feet!
Long caverns, winding within caverns, spread
On either side their labyrinths; all dark,
Save where the light falls glimmering on huge bones,
In mingled multitudes. Ere yet we ask
Whose bones, and of what animals they formed
The structure, when no human voice was heard
In all this isle; look upward to the roof
That silent drips, and has for ages dripped,
From which, like icicles, the stalactites
Depend: then ask of the geologist,
How nature, vaulting the rude chamber, scooped
Its vast recesses; he with learning vast
Will talk of limestone rock, of stalactites,
And oolites, and hornblende, and graywacke—
With sounds almost as craggy as the rock
Of which he speaks—feldspar, and gneis, and schorl!
But let us learn of this same troglodyte,
Who guides us through the winding labyrinth,
The erudite "Professor" of the cave,
Not of the college; stagyrite of bones.
He leads, with flickering candle, through the heaps
Himself has piled, and placed in various forms,
Grotesque arrangement, while the cave itself
Seems but his element of breathing! Look!
This humereus is that of the wild ox.
The very candle, as with sympathy,
Flares while he speaks, in glimmering wonderment!
But who can mark these visible remains,
Nor pause to think how awful, and how true,
The dread event they speak! What monuments
Hath man, since then, the lord, the emmet, raised

On earth! He hath built pyramids, and said,
Stand there! and in their solitude they stood,
Whilst, like the camel's shadow on the sands
Beneath them years and ages passed. He said,
My name shall never die! and like the God
Of silence, with his finger on his lip,
Oblivion mocked, then pointed to a tomb,
'Mid vast and winding vaults, without a name.
Where art thou, Thebes? The chambers of the dead
Echo, Behold! and twice ten thousand men,
Even in their march of rapine and of blood,
Involuntary halted, at the sight
Of thy majestic wreck, for many, a league—
Sphynxes, colossal fanes, and obelisks—
Pale in the morning sun! Ambition sighed
A moment, and passed on. In this rude isle,
The Druid altars frowned; and still they stand,
As silent as the barrows at their feet,
Yet tell the same stern tale. Soldier of Rome,
Art thou come hither to this land remote
Hid in the ocean-waste? Thy chariot wheels
Rung on that road below!—Cohorts, and turms,
With their centurions, in long file appear,
Their golden eagles glittering to the sun,
O'er the last line of spears; and standard-flags
Wave, and the trumpets sounding to advance,
And shields, and helms, and crests, and chariots, mark
The glorious march of Cæsar's soldiery,
Firing the gray horizon! They are passed!
And, like a gleam of glory, perishing,
Leave but a name behind! So passes man,
An armed spectre o'er a field of blood,
And vanishes; and other armed shades
Pass by, red battle hurtling as they pass.
The Saxon kings have strewed their palaces
From Thames to Tyne. But, lo! the sceptre shakes;
The Dane, remorseless as the hurricane
That sweeps his native cliffs, harries the land!
What terror strode before his track of blood!
What hamlets mourned his desultory march,
When on the circling hills, along the sea,
The beacon-flame shone nightly! He has passed!
Now frowns the Norman victor on his throne,
And every cottage shrouds its lonely fire,
As the sad curfew sounds. Yet Piety,
With new-inspiring energies, awoke,
And ampler polity: in woody vales,
In unfrequented wilds, and forest-glens,

The towers of the sequestered abbey shone,
As when the pinnacles of Glaston-Fane
First met the morning light. The parish church,
Then too, exulting o'er the ruder cross,
Upsprung, till soon the distant village peal
Flings out its music, where the tapering spire
Adds a new picture to the sheltered vale.
Uphill, thy rock, where sits the lonely church,
Above the sands, seems like the chronicler
Of other times, there left to tell the tale!
But issuing from the cave, look round, behold
How proudly the majestic Severn rides
On to the sea; how gloriously in light
It rides! Along this solitary ridge,
Where smiles, but rare, the blue campanula,
Among the thistles and gray stones that peep
Through the thin herbage, to the highest point
Of elevation, o'er the vale below,
Slow let us climb. First look upon that flower,
The lowly heath-bell, smiling at our feet.
How beautiful it smiles alone! The Power
That bade the great sea roar, that spread the heavens,
That called the sun from darkness, decked that flower,
And bade it grace this bleak and barren hill.
Imagination, in her playful mood,
Might liken it to a poor village maid,
Lowly, but smiling in her lowliness,
And dressed so neatly as if every day
Were Sunday. And some melancholy bard
Might, idly musing, thus discourse to it:—
Daughter of Summer, who dost linger here,
Decking the thistly turf, and arid hill,
Unseen, let the majestic dahlia
Glitter, an empress, in her blazonry
Of beauty; let the stately lily shine,
As snow-white as the breast of the proud swan
Sailing upon the blue lake silently,
That lifts her tall neck higher as she views
Her shadow in the stream! Such ladies bright
May reign unrivalled in their proud parterres!
Thou wouldst not live with them; but if a voice,
Fancy, in shaping mood, might give to thee,
To the forsaken primrose thou wouldst say—
Come, live with me, and we two will rejoice:
Nor want I company; for when the sea
Shines in the silent moonlight, elves and fays,
Gentle and delicate as Ariel,
That do their spiritings on these wild holts,

Circle me in their dance, and sing such songs
As human ear ne'er heard! But cease the strain,
Lest wisdom and severer truth should chide.
Behind that windmill, sailing round and round,
Like days on days revolving, Bleadon lies,
Where first I pondered on the grammar-lore,
Sad as the spelling-book, beneath the roof
Of its secluded parsonage; Brean Down
Emerges o'er the edge of Hutton Hill,
Just seen in paler light! And Weston there,
Where I remember a few cottages
Sprinkling the sand, uplifts its tower, and shines,
As if in conscious beauty, o'er the scene.
And I have seen a far more welcome sight,
The living line of population stream—
Children, and village maids, and gray old men—
Stream o'er the sands to church: such change has been
In the brief compass of one hastening life!
And yet that hill, the light, is to my eyes
Familiar as those sister isles that sit
In the mid channel! Look, how calm they sit,
As listening each to the tide's rocking roar!
Of different aspects—this, abrupt and high,
And desolate, and cold, and bleak, uplifts
Its barren brow—barren, but on its steep
One native flower is seen, the peony;
One flower, which smiles in sunshine or in storm,
There sits companionless, but yet not sad:
She has no sister of the summer-field,
None to rejoice with her when spring returns,
None that, in sympathy, may bend its head,
When evening winds blow hollow o'er the rock,
In autumn's gloom! So Virtue, a fair flower,
Blooms on the rock of Care, and, though unseen,
So smiles in cold seclusion; while, remote
From the world's flaunting fellowship, it wears,
Like hermit Piety, one smile of peace,
In sickness or in health, in joy or tears,
In summer days or cold adversity;
And still it feels Heaven's breath, reviving, steal
On its lone breast; feels the warm blessedness
Of Heaven's own light about it, though its leaves
Are wet with evening tears!
Yonder island
Seems not so desolate, nor frowns aloof,
As if from human kind. The lighthouse there,
Through the long winter night, shows its pale fire;
And three forgotten mounds mark the rude graves,

None knows of whom; but those of men who breathed,
And bore their part in life, and looked to Heaven,
As man looks now!—they died and left no name!
Fancy might think, amid the wilderness
Of waves, they sought to hide from human eyes
All memory of their fortunes. Till the trump
Of doom, they rest unknown. But mark that hill—
Where Kewstoke seems to creep into the sea,
Thy abbey, Woodspring, rose. Wild is the spot;
And there three mailed murderers retired,
To the last point of land. There they retired,
And there they knelt upon the ground, and cried,
Bury us 'mid the waves, where none may know
The whispered secret of a deed of blood!
No stone is o'er those graves:—the sullen tide,
As it flows by and sounds along the shore,
Seems moaningly to say, Pray for our souls!
Nor other "Miserere" have they had
At eve, nor other orison at morn.
Thou hast put on thy mildest look to-day,
Thou mighty element! Solemn, and still,
And motionless, and touched with softer light,
And without noise, lies all thy long expanse.
Thou seemest now as calm, as if a child
Might dally with thy playfulness, and stand,
The weak winds lifting gently its light hair;
Upon thy margin, watching one by one
The long waves, breaking slow, with such a sound
As Silence, in her dreamy mood, might love,
When she more softly breathed, fearing a breath
Might mar thy placidness!
Oh, treachery!
So still, and like a giant in his strength
Reposing, didst thou lie, when the fond sire
One moment looked, and saw his blithsome boys
Gay on the sands, one moment, and the next,
Heart-stricken and bereft, by the same surge,
Stood in his desolation;—for he looked,
And thought how he had blessed them in their sleep,
And the next moment they were borne away,
Snatched by the circling surge, and seen no more;
While morning shone, and not a ripple told
How terrible and dark a deed was done!
And so the seas were hushed, and not a cloud
Marred the pale moonlight, save that, here and there,
Wandering far off, some feathery shreds were seen,
As the sole orb, above the lighthouse, held
Its course in loveliness; and not a sound

Came from the distant deep, save that, at times,
Amid the noise of human merriment,
The ear might seem to catch a low faint moan,
A boding sound, as of a dying dirge,
From the sunk rocks; while all was still beside,
And every star seemed listening in its watch;
When the gay packet-bark, to Erin bound,
Resounding with the laugh and song, went on!
Look! she is gone! O God! she is gone down,
With her light-hearted company; gone down,
And all at once is still, save, on the mast,
Just peering o'er the waters, the wild shrieks
Of three, at times, are heard! They, when the dead
Were round them, floating on the moonlight wave,
Kept there their dismal watch till morning dawned,
And to the living world were then restored!

PART SECOND

REFLECTIONS ON THE MORAL AND RELIGIOUS STATE OF PARISHES, PAST AND PRESENT

A shower, even while we gaze, steals o'er the scene,
Shrouding it, and the sea-view is shout out,
Save where, beyond the holms, one thread of light
Hangs, and a pale and sunny stream shoots on,
O'er the dim vapours, faint and far away,
Like Hope's still light beyond the storms of Time.
Come, let us rest a while in this rude seat!
I was a child when first I heard the sound
Of the great sea. 'Twas night, and journeying far,
We were belated on our road, 'mid scenes
New and unknown,—a mother and her child,
Now first in this wide world a wanderer:—
My father came, the pastor of the church
That crowns the high hill crest, above the sea;
When, as the wheels went slow, and the still night
Seemed listening, a low murmur met the ear,
Not of the winds:—my mother softly said,
Listen! it is the sea! With breathless awe,
I heard the sound, and closer pressed her hand.
Much of the sea, in infant wonderment,
I oft had heard, and of the shipwrecked man,
Who sees, on some lone isle, day after day,
The sun sink o'er the solitude of waves,
Like Crusoe; and the tears would start afresh,
Whene'er my mother kissed my cheek, and told

The story of that desolate wild man,
And how the speaking bird, when he returned
After long absence to his cave forlorn,
Said, as in tones of human sympathy,
Poor Robin Crusoe!
Thoughts like these arose,
When first I heard, at night, the distant sound,
Great Ocean, "of thy everlasting voice!"
Where the white parsonage, among the trees,
Peeped out, that night I restless passed. The sea
Filled all my thoughts; and when slow morning came,
And the first sunbeam streaked the window-pane,
I rose unnoticed, and with stealthy pace,
Straggling along the village green, explored
Alone my fearful but adventurous way;
When, having turned the hedgerow, I beheld,
For the first time, thy glorious element,
Old Ocean, glittering in the beams of morn,
Stretching far off, and, westward, without bound,
Amid thy sole dominion, rocking loud!
Shivering I stood, and tearful; and even now,
When gathering years have marked my look,—even now
I feel the deep impression of that hour,
As but of yesterday!
Spirit of Time,
A moment pause, and I will speak to thee!
Dark clouds are round thee; but, lo! Memory waves
Her wand,—the clouds disperse, as the gray rack
Disperses while we gaze, and light steals out,
While the gaunt phantom almost seems to drop
His scythe! Now shadows of the past, distinct,
Are thronging round; the voices of the dead
Are heard; and, lo! the very smoke goes up—
For so it seems—from yonder tenement,
Where leads the slender pathway to the door.
Enter that small blue parlour: there sits one,
A female, and a child is in her arms;
A child leans at her side, intent to show
A pictured book, and looks upon her face;
One, from the green, comes with a cowslip ball;
And one, a hero, sits sublime and horsed,
Upon a rocking-steed, from Banwell-fair;
This, drives his tiny wheel-barrow, without,
On the green garden-sward; whilst one, apart,
Sighs o'er his solemn task—the spelling-book—
Half moody, half in tears. Some lines of thought
Are on that matron's brow; yet placidness,
Such as resigned religion gives, is there,

Mingled with sadness; for who e'er beheld,
Without one stealing sigh, a progeny
Of infants clustering round maternal knees,
Nor felt some boding fears, how they might fare
In the wide world, when they who loved them most
Were silent in their graves!
Nay! pass not on,
Till thou hast marked a book—the leaf turned down—
Night Thoughts on Death and Immortality!
This book, my mother! in the weary hours
Of life, in every care, in every joy,
Was thy companion: next to God's own Word,
The book that bears this name, thou didst revere,
Leaving a stain of tears upon the page,
Whose lessons, with a more emphatic truth,
Touched thine own heart!
That heart has long been still!
But who is he, of aspect more severe,
Yet with a manly kindness in his mien,
He, who o'erlooks yon sturdy labourer
Delving the glebe! My father as he lived!
That father, and that mother, "earth to earth,
And dust to dust," the inevitable doom
Hath long consigned! And where is he, the son,
Whose future fate they pondered with a sigh?
Long, nor unprosperous, has been his way
Through life's tumultuous scenes, who, when a child,
Played in that garden platform in the sun;
Or loitered o'er the common, and pursued
The colts among the sand-hills; or, intent
On hardier enterprise, his pumpkin-ship,
New-rigged, and buoyant, with its tiny sail,
Launched on the garden pond; or stretched his hand,
At once forgetting all this glorious toil,
When the bright butterfly came wandering by.
But never will that day pass from his mind,
When, scarcely breathing for delight, at Wells,
He saw the horsemen of the clock ride round,
As if for life; and ancient Blandifer,
Seated aloft, like Hermes, in his chair
Complacent as when first he took his seat,
Some hundred years ago; saw him lift up,
As if old Time was cowering at his feet,
Solemn lift up his mace, and strike the bell,
Himself for ever silent in his seat.
How little thought I then, the hour would come,
When the loved prelate of that beauteous fane,
At whose command I write, might placidly

Smile on this picture, in my future verse,
When Blandifer had struck so many hours
For me, his poet, in this vale of years,
Himself unchanged and solemn as of yore!
My father was the pastor, and the friend
Of all who, living then—the scene is closed—
Now silent in that rocky churchyard sleep,
The aged and the young! A village then
Was not as villages are now. The hind,
Who delved, or "jocund drove his team a-field,"
Had then an independence in his look
And heart; and, plodding on his lowly path,
Disdained a parish dole, content, though poor.
He was the village monitor: he taught
His children to be good, and read their book,
And in the gallery took his Sunday place,—
To-morrow, with the bee, to work.
So passed
His days of cheerful, independent toil;
And when the pastor came that way, at eve,
He had a ready present for the child
Who read his book the best; and that poor child
Remembered it, when, treading the same path
In which his father trod, he so grew up
Contented, till old Time had blanched his locks,
And he was borne—whilst the bell tolled—to sleep
In the same churchyard where his father slept!
His daughter walked content, and innocent
As lovely, in her lowly path. She turned
The hour-glass, while the humming wheel went round,
Or went "a-Maying" o'er the fields in spring,
Leading her little brother by the hand,
Along the village lane, and o'er the stile,
To gather cowslips; and then home again,
To turn her wheel, contented, through the day.
Or, singing low, bend where her brother slept,
Rocking the cradle, to "sweet William's grave!"
No lure could tempt her from the woodbine shed,
Where she grew up, and folded first her hands
In infant prayer: yet oft a tear would steal
Down her young cheek, to think how desolate
That home would be when her poor mother died;
Still praying that she ne'er might cause a pain,
Undutiful, to "bring down her gray hairs
With sorrow to the grave!"
Now mark this scene!
The fuming factory's polluted air
Has stained the country! See that rural nymph,

An infant in her arms! She claims the dole
From the cold parish, which her faithless swain
Denies: he stands aloof, with clownish leer;
The constable behind—and mark his brow—
Beckons the nimble clerk; the justice, grave,
Turns from his book a moment, with a look
Of pity, signs the warrant for her pay,
A weekly eighteen pence; she, unabashed,
Slides from the room, and not a transient blush,
Far less the accusing tear, is on her cheek!
A different scene comes next: That village maid
Approaches timidly, yet beautiful;
A tear is on her lids, when she looks down
Upon her sleeping child. Her heart was won,
The wedding-day was fixed, the ring was bought!
'Tis the same story—Colin was untrue!
He ruined, and then left her to her fate.
Pity her, she has not a friend on earth,
And that still tear speaks to all human hearts
But his, whose cruelty and treachery
Caused it to flow! So crime still follows crime.
Ask we the cause? See, where those engines heave,
That spread their giant arms o'er all the land!
The wheel is silent in the vale! Old age
And youth are levelled by one parish law!
Ask why that maid, all day, toils in the field,
Associate with the rude and ribald clown,
Even in the shrinking April of her youth?
To earn her loaf, and eat it by herself.
Parental love is smitten to the dust;
Over a little smoke the aged sire
Holds his pale hands—and the deserted hearth
Is cheerless as his heart: but Piety
Points to the Bible! Shut the book again:
The ranter is the roving gospel now,
And each his own apostle! Shut the book:
A locust-swarm of tracts darken its light,
And choke its utterance; while a Babel-rout
Of mock-religionists, turn where we will,
Have drowned the small still voice, till Piety,
Sick of the din, retires to pray alone.
But though abused Religion, and the dole
Of pauper-pay, and vomitories huge
Of smoke, are each a steam-engine of crime,
Polluting, far and wide, the wholesome air,
And withering life's green verdure underneath,
Full many a poor and lowly flower of want
Has Education nursed, like a pure rill,

Winding through desert glens, and bade it live
To grace the cottage with its mantling sweets.
There was a village girl, I knew her well,
From five years old and upwards; all her friends
Were dead, and she was to the workhouse left,
And there a witness to such sounds profane
As might turn virtue pale! When Sunday came,
Assembled with the children of the poor,
Upon the lawn of my own parsonage,
She stood among them: they were taught to read
In companies and groups, upon the green,
Each with its little book; her lighted eyes
Shone beautiful where'er they turned; her form
Was graceful; but her book her sole delight!
Instructed thus she went a serving-maid
Into the neighbouring town,—ah! who shall guide
A friendless maid, so beautiful and young,
From life's contagions! But she had been taught
The duties of her humble lot, to pray
To God, and that one heavenly Father's eye
Was over rich and poor! On Sunday night,
She read her Bible, turning still away
From those who flocked, inflaming and inflamed,
To nightly meetings; but she never closed
Her eyes, or raised them to the light of morn,
Without a prayer to Him who "bade the sun
Go forth," a giant, from his eastern gate!
No art, no bribe, could lure her steps astray
From the plain path, and lessons she had learned,
A village child. She is a mother now,
And lives to prove the blessings and the fruits
Of moral duty, on the poorest child,
When duty, and when sober piety,
Impressing the young heart, go hand in hand.
No villager was then a disputant
In Calvinistic and contentious creeds;
No pale mechanic, from a neighbouring sink
Of steam and rank debauchery and smoke,
Crawled forth upon a Sunday morn, with looks
Saddening the very sunshine, to instruct
The parish poor in evangelic lore;
To teach them to cast off, "as filthy rags,"
Good works! and listen to such ministers,
Who all (be sure) "are worthy of their hire;"
Who only preach for good of their poor souls,
That they may turn "from darkness unto light,"
And, above all, fly, as the gates of hell,
Morality! and Baal's steeple house,

Where, without "heart-work," Doctor Littlegrace
Drones his dull requiem to the snoring clerk!"
True; he who drawls his heartless homily
For one day's work, and plods, on wading stilts,
Through prosing paragraphs, with inference,
Methodically dull, as orthodox,
Enforcing sagely that we all must die
When God shall call—oh, what a pulpit drone
Is he! The blue fly might as well preach "Hum,"
And "so conclude!"
But save me from the sight
Of curate fop, half jockey and half clerk,
The tandem-driving Tommy of a town,
Disdaining books, omniscient of a horse,
Impatient till September comes again,
Eloquent only of "the pretty girl
With whom he danced last night!" Oh! such a thing
Is worse than the dull doctor, who performs
Duly his stinted task, and then to sleep,
Till Sunday asks another homily
Against all innovations of the age,
Mad missionary zeal, and Bible clubs,
And Calvinists and Evangelicals!
Yes! Evangelicals! Oh, glorious word!
But who deserves that awful name? Not he
Who spits his puny Puritanic spite
On harmless recreation; who reviles
All who, majestic in their distant scorn,
Bear on in silence their calm Christian course.
He only is the Evangelical
Who holds in equal scorn dogmas and dreams,
The Shibboleth of saintly magazines,
Decked with most grim and godly visages;
The cobweb sophistry, or the dark code
Of commentators, who, with loathsome track,
Crawl o'er a text, or on the lucid page,
Beaming with heavenly love and God's own light,
Sit like a nightmare! Soon a deadly mist
Creeps o'er our eyes and heart, till angel forms
Turn into hideous phantoms, mocking us,
Even when we look for comfort at the spring
And well of life, while dismal voices cry,
Death! Reprobation! Woe! Eternal woe!
He only is the Evangelical
Who from the human commentary turns
With tranquil scorn, and nearer to his heart
Presses the Bible, till repentant tears,
In silence, wet his cheek, and new-born faith,

And hope, and charity, with radiant smile,
Visit his heart,—all pointing to the cross!
He only is the Evangelical,
Who, with eyes fixed upon that spectacle,
Christ and him crucified, with ardent hope,
And holier feelings, lifts his thoughts from earth,
And cries, My Father! Meantime, his whole heart
Is on God's Word: he preaches Faith, and Hope,
And Charity,—these three, and not that one!
And Charity, the greatest of these three!
Give me an Evangelical like this! But now
The blackest crimes in tract-religion's code
Are moral virtues! Spare the prodigal,—
He may awake when God shall "call;" but, hell,
Roll thy avenging flames, to swallow up
The son who never left his father's home
Lest he should trust to morals when he dies!
Let him not lay the unction to his soul,
That his upbraiding conscience tells no tale
At that dread hour; bid him confess his sin,
The greater that, with humble hope, he looks
Back on a well-spent life! Bid him confess
That he hath broken all God's holy laws,—
In vain hath he done justly,—loved, in vain,
Mercy, and hath walked humbly with his God!
These are mere works; but faith is everything,
And all in all! The Christian code contains
No "if" or "but!" Let tabernacles ring,
And churches too, with sanctimonious strains
Baneful as these; and let such strains be heard
Through half the land; and can we shut our eyes,
And, sadly wondering, ask the cause of crimes,
When infidelity stands lowering here,
With open scorn, and such a code as this,
So baneful, withers half the charities
Of human hearts! Oh! dear is Mercy's voice
To man, a mourner in the vale of sin
And death: how dear the still small voice of Faith,
That bids him raise his look beyond the clouds
That hang o'er this dim earth; but he who tears
Faith from her heavenly sisterhood, denies
The gospel, and turns traitor to the cause
He has engaged to plead. Come, Faith, and Hope,
And Charity! how dear to the sad heart,
The consolations and the glorious views
That animate the Christian in his course!
But save, oh! save me from the tract-led Miss,
Who trots to every Bethel club, and broods

O'er some black missionary's monstrous tale,
Reckless of want around her!
But the priest,
Who deems the Almighty frowns upon his throne,
Because two pair of harmless dowagers,
Whose life has passed without a stain, beguile
An evening hour with cards; who deems that hell
Burns fiercer for a saraband; that thou—
Thou, my sweet Shakspeare—thou, whose touch awakes
The inmost heart of virtuous sympathy,—
Thou, O divinest poet! at whose voice
Sad Pity weeps, or guilty Terror drops
The blood-stained dagger from his palsied hand,—
That thou art pander to the criminal!
He who thus edifies his Christian flock,
Moves, more than even the Bethel-trotting Miss,
My pity, my aversion, and my scorn.
Cry aloud!—Oh, speak in thunder to the soul
That sleeps in sin! Harrow the inmost heart
Of murderous intent, till dew-drops stand
Upon his haggard brow! Call conscience up,
Like a stern spectre, whose dim finger points
To dark misdeeds of yore! Wither the arm
Of the oppressor, at whose feet the slave
Crouches, and pleading lifts his fettered hands!
Thou violator of the innocent
Hide thee! Hence! hide thee in the deepest cave,
From man's indignant sight! Thou hypocrite!
Trample in dust thy mask, nor cry faith, faith,
Making it but a hollow tinkling sound,
That stirs not the foul heart! Horrible wretch!
Look not upon the face of that sweet child,
With thoughts which hell would tremble to conceive!
Oh, shallow, and oh, senseless! In a world
Where rank offences turn the good man pale,
Who leave the Christian's sternest code, to vent
Their petty ire on petty trespasses,
If trespasses they are;—when the wide world
Groans with the burthen of offence; when crimes
Stalk on, with front defying, o'er the land,
Whilst, her own cause betraying, Christian zeal
Thus swallows camels, straining at a gnat!
Therefore, without a comment, or a note,
We love the Bible; and we prize the more
The spirit of its pure unspotted page,
As pure from the infectious breath that stains,
Like a foul fume, its hallowed light, we hail
The radiant car of heaven, amidst the clouds

Of mortal darkness, and of human mist,
Sole, as the sun in heaven!
Oh! whilst the car
Of God's own glory rolls along in light,
We join the loud song of the Christian host,
(All puny systems shrinking from the blaze),
Hosannah to the car of light! Roll on!
Saldanna's rocks have echoed to the hymns
Of Faith, and Hope, and Charity! Roll on!
Till the wild wastes of inmost Africa,
Where the long Niger's track is lost, respond,
Hosannah to the car of light! Roll on!
From realm to realm, from shore to farthest shore,
O'er dark pagodas, and huge idol-fanes,
That frown along the Ganges' utmost stream,
Till the poor widow, from the burning pile
Starting, shall lift her hands to heaven, and weep
That she has found a Saviour, and has heard
The sounds of Christian love! Oh, horrible!
The pile is smoking!—the bamboos lie there,
That held her down when the last struggle shook
The blazing pile! Hasten, O car of light!
Alas for suffering nature! Juggernaut,
Armed, in his giant car goes also forth,
Goes forth amid his red and reeling priests,
While thousands gasp and die beneath the wheels,
As they go groaning on, 'mid cries, and drums,
And flashing cymbals, and delirious songs
Of tinkling dancing girls, and all the rout
Of frantic superstition! Turn away!
And is not Juggernaut himself with us?
Not only cold insidious sophistry
Comes, blinking with its taper-fume, to light,
If so he may, the sun in the mid heaven!
Not only blind and hideous blasphemy
Scowls in his cloak, and mocks the glorious orb,
Ascending, in its silence, o'er a world
Of sin and sorrow; but a hellish brood
Of imps, and fiends, and phantoms, ape the form
Of godliness, till godliness itself
Seems but a painted monster, and a name
For darker crimes, at which the shuddering heart
Shrinks; while the ranting rout, as they march on,
Mock Heaven with hymns, till, see! pale Belial
Sighs o'er a filthy tract, and Moloch marks,
With gouts of blood, his brandished magazine!
Start, monster, from the dismal dream! Look up!
Oh! listen to the apostolic voice,

That, like a voice from heaven, proclaims, To faith
Add virtue! There is no mistaking here;
Whilst moral education by the hand
Shall lead the children to the house of God,
Nor sever Christian faith from Christian love.
If we would see the fruits of charity,
Look at that village group, and paint the scene!
Surrounded by a clear and silent stream,
Where the swift trout shoots from the sudden ray,
A rural mansion on the level lawn
Uplifts its ancient gables, whose slant shade
Is drawn, as with a line, from roof to porch,
Whilst all the rest is sunshine. O'er the trees
In front, the village church, with pinnacles
And light gray tower, appears; whilst to the right,
An amphitheatre of oaks extends
Its sweep, till, more abrupt, a wooded knoll,
Where once a castle frowned, closes the scene.
And see! an infant troop, with flags and drum,
Are marching o'er that bridge, beneath the woods,
On to the table spread upon the lawn,
Raising their little hands when grace is said;
Whilst she who taught them to lift up their hearts
In prayer, and to "remember, in their youth,"
God, "their Creator," mistress of the scene
(Whom I remember once as young), looks on,
Blessing them in the silence of her heart.
And we too bless them. Oh! away, away!
Cant, heartless cant, and that economy,
Cold, and miscalled "political," away!
Let the bells ring—a Puritan turns pale
To hear the festive sound: let the bells ring—
A Christian loves them; and this holiday
Remembers him, while sighs unbidden steal,
Of life's departing and departed days,
When he himself was young, and heard the bells,
In unison with feelings of his heart—
His first pure Christian feelings, hallowing
The harmonious sound!
And, children, now rejoice,—
Now, for the holidays of life are few;
Nor let the rustic minstrel tune, in vain,
The cracked church-viol, resonant to-day
Of mirth, though humble! Let the fiddle scrape
Its merriment, and let the joyous group
Dance in a round, for soon the ills of life
Will come! Enough, if one day in the year,
If one brief day, of this brief life, be given

To mirth as innocent as yours! But, lo!
That ancient woman, leaning on her staff!
Pale, on her crutch she rests one withered hand;
One withered hand, which Gerard Dow might paint,
Even its blue veins! And who is she? The nurse
Of the fair mistress of the scene: she led
Her tottering steps in infancy—she spelt
Her earliest lesson to her; and she now
Leans from that open window, while she thinks—
When summer comes again, the turf will lie
On my cold breast; but I rejoice to see
My child thus leading on the progeny
Of her poor neighbours in the peaceful path
Of humble virtue! I shall be at rest,
Perhaps, when next they meet; but my last prayer
Is with them, and the mistress of this home.
"The innocent are gay," gay as the lark
That sings in morn's first sunshine; and why not?
But may they ne'er forget, as life steals on,
In age, the lessons they have learned in youth!
How false the charge, how foul the calumny
On England's generous aristocracy,
That, wrapped in sordid, selfish apathy,
They feel not for the poor!
Ask, is it true?
Lord of the whirling wheels, the charge is false!
Ten thousand charities adorn the land,
Beyond thy cold conception, from this source.
What cottage child but has been neatly clad,
And taught its earliest lesson, from their care?
Witness that schoolhouse, mantled with festoon
Of various plants, which fancifully wreath
Its window-mullions, and that rustic porch,
Whence the low hum of infant voices blend
With airs of spring, without. Now, all alive,
The green sward rings with play, among the shrubs—
Hushed the long murmur of the morning task,
Before the pensive matron's desk!
But turn,
And mark that aged widow! By her side
Is God's own Word; and, lo! the spectacles
Are yet upon the page. Her daughter kneels
And prays beside her! Many years have shed
Their snow so silently and softly down
Upon her head, that Time, as if to gaze,
Seems for a moment to suspend his flight
Onward, in reverence to those few gray hairs,
That steal beneath her cap, white as its snow.

Whilst the expiring lamp is kept alive,
Thus feebly, by a duteous daughter's love,
Her last faint prayer, ere all is dark on earth,
Will to the God of heaven ascend, for those
Whose comforts smoothed her silent bed.
And thou,
Witness Elysian Tempe of Stourhead!
Oh, not because, with bland and gentle smile,
Adding a radiance to the look of age,
Like eve's still light, thy liberal master spreads
His lettered treasures;—not because his search
Has dived the Druid mound, illustrating
His country's annals, and the monuments
Of darkest ages;—not because his woods
Wave o'er the dripping cavern of Old Stour,
Where classic temples gleam along the edge
Of the clear waters, winding beautiful;—
Oh! not because the works of breathing art,
Of Poussin, Rubens, Rembrandt, Gainsborough,
Start, like creations, from the silent walls;
To thee, this tribute of respect and love,
Beloved, benevolent, and generous Hoare,
Grateful I pay;—but that, when thou art dead
(Late may it be!) the poor man's tear will fall,
And his voice falter, when he speaks of thee.
And witness thou, magnificent abode,
Where virtuous Ken, with his gray hairs and shroud,
Came, for a shelter from the world's rude storm,
In his old age, leaving his palace-throne,
Having no spot where he might lay his head,
In all the earth! Oh, witness thou, the seat
Of his first friend, his friend from schoolboy days!
Oh! witness thou, if one who wanted bread
Has not found shelter there; if one poor man
Has been deserted in his hour of need;
Or one poor child been left without a guide,
A father, an instructor, and a friend;
In him, the pastor, and distributor
Of bounties large, yet falling silently
As dews on the cold turf! And witness thou,
Marston, the seat of my kind, honoured friend—
My kind and honoured friend, from youthful days.
Then wandering on the banks of Rhine, we saw
Cities and spires, beneath the mountains blue,
Gleaming; or vineyards creep from rock to rock;
Or unknown castles hang, as if in clouds:
Or heard the roaring of the cataract,
Far off, beneath the dark defile or gloom

Of ancient forests; till behold, in light,
Foaming and flashing, with enormous sweep,
Through the rent rocks—where, o'er the mist of spray
The rainbow, like a fairy in her bower,
Is sleeping, while it roars—that volume vast,
White, and with thunder's deafening roar, comes down.
Live long, live happy, till thy journey close,
Calm as the light of day! Yet witness thou,
The seat of noble ancestry, the seat
Of science, honoured by the name of Boyle,
Though many sorrows, since we met in youth,
Have pressed thy generous master's manly heart,
Witness, the partner of his joys and griefs;
Witness the grateful tenantry, the home
Of the poor man, the children of that school—
Still warm benevolence sits smiling there.
And witness, the fair mansion, on the edge
Of those chalk hills, which, from my garden walk,
Daily I see, whose gentle mistress droops
With her own griefs, yet never turns her look
From others' sorrows; on whose lids the tear
Shines yet more lovely than the light of youth.
And many a cottage-garden smiles, whose flowers
Invite the music of the morning bee.
And many a fireside has shot out, at eve,
Its light upon the old man's withered hand
And pallid cheek from their benevolence—
Sad as is still the parish-pauper's home—
Who shed around their patrimonial seats
The light of heaven-descending Charity.
And every feeling of the Christian heart
Would rise accusing, could I pass unsung,
Thee, fair as Charity's own form, who late
Didst stand beneath the porch of that gray fane,
Soliciting a mite from all who passed,
With such a smile, as to refuse would seem
To do a wrong to Charity herself.
How many blessings, silent and unheard,
The mistress of the lonely parsonage
Dispenses, when she takes her daily round
Among the aged and the sick, whose prayers
And blessings are her only recompense!
How many pastors, by cold obloquy
And senseless hate reviled, tread the same path
Of charity in silence, taught by Him
Who was reviled not to revile again;
And leaving to a righteous God their cause!
Come, let us, with the pencil in our hand,

Portray a character. What book is this?
Rector of Overton! I know him not;
But well I know the Vicar, and a man
More worthy of that name, and worthier still
To grace a higher station of our Church,
None knows;—a friend and father to the poor,
A scholar, unobtrusive, yet profound,
"As e'er my conversation coped withal;"
His piety unvarnished, but sincere.
Killarney's lake, and Scotia's hills, have heard
His summer-wandering reed; nor on the themes
Of hallowed inspiration has his harp
Been silent, though ten thousand jangling strings—
When all are poets in this land of song,
And every field chinks with its grasshopper—
Have well-nigh drowned the tones; but poesy
Mingles, at eventide, with many a mood
Of stirring fancy, on his silent heart
When o'er those bleak and barren downs, in rain
Or sunshine, where the giant Wansdeck sweeps,
Homewards he bends his solitary way.
Live long; and late may the old villager
Look on thy stone, amid the churchyard grass,
Remembering years of kindness, and the tongue,
Eloquent of his Maker, when he sat
At church, and heard the undivided code
Of apostolic truth—of hope, of faith,
Of charity—the end and test of all.
Live long; and though I proudly might recall
The names of many friends—like thee, sincere
And pious, and in solitude adorned
With rare accomplishments—this grateful praise
Accept, congenial to the poet's theme;
For well I know, haply when I am dead,
And in my shroud, whene'er thy homeward path
Lies o'er those hills, and thou shalt cast a look
Back on our garden-slope, and Bremhill tower,
Thou wilt remember me, and many a day
There passed in converse and sweet harmony.
A truce to satire, and to harsh reproof,
Severer arguments, that have detained
The unwilling Muse too long:—come, while the clouds
Work heavy and the winds at intervals,
Pipe, and at intervals sink in a sigh,
As breathed o'er sounds and shadows of the past—
Change we our style and measure, to relate
A village tale of a poor Cornish maid,
And of her prayer-book. It is sad, but true;

And simply told, though not in lady phrase
Of modish song, may touch some gentle heart,
And wake an interest, when description fails.

PART THIRD

THE MAIDEN'S CURSE

I subjoin the plain narrative of the singular event on which this tale is founded, from Mr Polwhele, that the reader may see how far, poetically, I have departed from plain facts, and what I have thought it best to add for the sake of moral, picturesque, and poetical effect. The narrative is as follows:—

"October,. Thomas Thomas, aged . This man died of mental anguish, or what is called a broken heart. He lived in the village of Drannock, in the parish of Gwinnear, till an unhappy event occurred, which proved fatal to his peace of mind for more than eight years, and finally occasioned his death. He courted Elizabeth Thomas, of the same village, who was his first-cousin; and it was understood that they were under a matrimonial engagement. But in May , some little disagreement having happened between them, he, out of resentment, or from some other motive, paid great attention to another girl; and on Sunday the st of that month, in the afternoon, accompanied her to the Methodist meeting at Wall. During their absence, the slighted female, who was very beautiful in her person, but of an extremely irritable temper, took a rope and a common prayer-book, in which she had folded down the th Psalm, and, going into an adjacent field, hanged herself. Thomas, on his return from the preaching, inquired for Betsy; and being told she had not been seen for two or three hours, he exclaimed, 'Good God! she has destroyed herself!' which apprehension seems to show, either that she had threatened to commit suicide in consequence of his desertion, or that he dreaded it from a knowledge of the violence of her disposition. But when he saw that his fears were realised, and had read the psalm, so full of execrations, which she had pointed out to him, he cried out, 'I am ruined for ever and ever!' The very sight of this village and neighbourhood was now become insupportable, and he went to live at Marazion, hoping that a change of scene and social intercourse might expel those excruciating reflections which harrowed up his very soul, or at least render them less acute; but in this he appeared to be mistaken, for he found himself closely pursued by the evil demon

'Despair, whose torments no man, sure,
But lovers and the damned endure.'

"To hear the th Psalm would petrify him with horror, and therefore he would not attend divine service on the d day of the month; he dreaded to go near a reading school, lest he should hear the dreaded lesson. Whatever misfortunes befel him (and these were not a few, for he was several times hurt, and even maimed, in the mines in which he laboured), he still attributed them all to the malevolent agency of the deceased, and thought he could find allusions to the whole in the calamitous legacy which she had bequeathed him. When he slumbered, for he knew nothing of sound sleep, the injured girl appeared to his imagination, with such a countenance as she retained after the rash action, and the prayer-book in her hand, open at the hateful psalm; and he was frequently heard to cry out, 'Oh, my dear Betsy, shut the book, shut the book!' etc. With a mind so disturbed and deranged, though he could not reasonably expect much consolation from matrimony, yet imagining that the cares of a family might distract his thoughts from the miserable subject by which he was harassed both by day and night, he successively paid his addresses to many girls of Marazion; but they indignantly flew from him, and with a sneer asked him, whether he was desirous of bringing all the curses in the th Psalm on their heads? At length, however, he succeeded with one who had less superstition and more fortitude than the rest, and he led her to St Hilary church, to be married, January, ; but on the road thither, they were overtaken by a sudden and violent hurricane, such as those which not unfrequently happen in the vicinity of Mount's Bay; and he, suspecting that poor Betsy rode the whirlwind and directed the storm, was convulsed with terror, and was literally 'coupled with fear.' Such is the power of conscious guilt to impute accidental occurrences to the hand of vindictive justice, and so true is the observation of the poet,

'Judicium metuit sibi mens mali conscia justum.'

"He lived long enough to have a son and a daughter; but the corrosive worm within his breast preyed upon his vitals, and at length consumed all the powers of his body, as it had long before destroyed the tranquillity of his mind, and he was released from all his pangs, both mental and corporeal, on Friday, October , , and buried at St Hilary, the Sunday following, during evening service."

Oh! shut the book, dear Mary, shut the book!
So William cried, with wild and frantic look.
She whom he loved was in her shroud, nor pain
Nor grief can visit her sad heart again.
There is no sculptured tombstone at her head;
No rude memorial marks her lowly bed:
The village children, every holiday,
Round the green turf, in summer sunshine play;
And none, but those now bending to the tomb,
Remember Mary, lovely in her bloom!
Yet oft the hoary swain, when autumn sighs
Through the long grass, sees a dim form arise,
That hies in glimmering moonlight to the brook,
Its wan lips moving, in its hand a book.
So, like a bruised flower, and in the pride
Of youth and beauty, injured Mary died.
William some years survived, but years no trace
Of his sick heart's deep anguish could erase.
Still the dread spectre seemed to rise, and, worse,
Still in his ears rang the appalling curse!
While loud he cries, despair upon his look,
Oh! shut the book, my Mary, shut the book!
The sun is slowly westering now, and lo,
How beautiful steals out the humid bow,
A radiant arch! Listen, whilst I relate
William's dread judgment, and poor Mary's fate.
I think I see the pine, that, heavily
Swaying, yet seems as for the dead to sigh.
How many generations, since the day
Of its green pride, have passed, like leaves, away!
How many children of the hamlet played
Round its hoar trunk, who at its feet were laid,

Withered and gray old men! In life's first bloom
How many has it seen borne to the tomb!
But never one so sunk in hopeless woe
As she who lies in the cold grave below.
Her Sabbath-book, from which at church she prayed,
Was her poor father's, in that churchyard laid:
For Mary grew as beautiful in youth,
As taught at church the lore of heavenly truth.
What different passions in her bosom strove,
When first she heard the tale of village love!
The youth whose voice then won her partial ear,
A yeoman's son, had passed his twentieth year;
She scarce eighteen: her mother, with the care
Of boding age, oft whispered, Oh, beware!
For William was a thoughtless youth, and wild,
And like a colt unbroken, from a child:
At length, if not to serious thoughts awake,
He came to church, at least for Mary's sake.
Young Mary, while her father was alive,
Saw all things round the humble dwelling thrive;
Her widowed mother now was growing old,
And bit by bit their worldly goods were sold:
Mary remained, her mother's hope and pride!
How oft when she was sleeping by her side,
That mother waked, and kissed her cheek, with tears
Praying for blessings on her future years,—
When she, her mother, earthly trials o'er,
Should rest in the cold grave, to grieve no more!
But Mary to love's dream her heart resigned,
And gave to fancy all her youthful mind.
Shall I describe her! Didst thou never mark
A soft blue light, beneath eye-lashes dark?
Such was her eye's soft light;—her chestnut hair,
Light as she tripped, waved lighter to the air;
And, with her prayer-book, when on Sunday dressed,
Her looks a sweet but lowly grace expressed,
As modest as the violet at her breast.
Sometimes all day by her lone mother's side
She sat, and oft would turn, a tear to hide.
Where winds the brook, by yonder bordering wood,
Her mother's solitary cottage stood:
A few white pales in front, fenced from the road
The garden-plot, and poor but neat abode.
Before the window, 'mid the flowers of spring
A bee-hive hummed, whose bees were murmuring;
Beneath an ivied bank, abrupt and high,
A small clear well reflected bank and sky,
In whose translucent mirror, smooth and still,

From time to time, a small bird dipped its bill.
Here the first bluebell, and, of livelier hue,
The daffodil and polyanthus grew.
'Twas Mary's care a jessamine to train.
With small white blossoms, round the window-pane:
A rustic wicket opened to the meads,
Where a scant pathway to the hamlet leads:
And near, a water-wheel toiled round and round,
Dashing the o'ershot stream, with long continuous sound.
Beyond, when the brief shower had sailed away,
The tapering spire shone out in sunlight gray;
And o'er that mountain's northern point, to sight
Stretching far on, the main-sea rolled in light.
Enter: within, see everything how neat!
One book lies open on the window-seat,
The spectacles are on a leaf of Job:
There, mark, a map of the terrestrial globe;
And opposite, with its prolific stem,
The Christian's tree, and New Jerusalem;
Here, see a printed paper, to record
A veritable letter from our Lord:
Two books are on the window-ledge beneath,—
The Book of Prayer, and Drelincourt on Death:
Some cowslips, in a cup of china placed,
A painted shelf above the chimney graced:
Grown like its mistress old, with half-shut eyes,
Save when, at times, awaked by wandering flies,
Tib in the sunshine of the casement lies.
'Twas spring time now, with birds the garden rung,
And Mary's linnet at the window sung.
Whilst in the air the vernal music floats,
The cuckoo only joins his two sweet notes:
But those—oh! listen, for he sings more near—
So musical, so mellow, and so clear!
Not sweeter, where thy mighty waters sweep,
Missouri, through the night of forests deep,
Resounds, from glade to glade, from rock to hill,
While fervent harmonies the wild wood fill,
The solitary note of "whip-poor-will;"
Mary's old mother stops her wheel to say,
The cuckoo! hark! how sweet he sings to-day!
It is not long, not long to Whitsuntide,
And Mary then shall be a happy bride.
On Sunday morn, when a slant light was flung
Upon the tower, and the first peal was rung,
William and Mary smiling would repair,
Arm linked in arm, to the same house of prayer.
The bells will sound more merrily, he cried,

And gently pressed her hand, at Whitsuntide:
She checked the rising thoughts, and hung her head;
And Mary, ere one year had passed—was dead!
'Twas said, and many would the tale believe,
Her shrouded form was seen upon that eve,
When, gliding through the churchyard, they appear—
They who shall die within the coming year.
All pale, and strangely piteous, was her look,
Her right hand was stretched out, and held a book;
O'er it her wet hair dripped, while the moon cast
A cold wan light, as in her shroud she passed!
I cannot say if this were so, but late,
She went to Madern-stone, to learn her fate,
What there she heard ne'er came to human ears—
But from that hour she oft was seen in tears.
Mild zephyr breathes, the butterfly more bright
Strays, wavering, o'er the pales, in rainbow light;
The lamb, the colt, the blackbird in the brake,
Seem all the vernal feeling to partake;
The lark sings high in air, itself unseen,
The hasty swallow skims the village-green;
And all things seem, to the full heart, to bring
The blissful breathings of the world's first spring.
How lovely is the sunshine of May-morn!
The garden bee has wound his earliest horn,
Busied from flower to flower, as he would say,
Up! Mary! up this merry morn of May!
Now lads and lasses of the hamlet bore
Branches of blossomed thorn or sycamore;
And at her mother's porch a garland hung,
While thus their rural roundelay they sung:—

And we were up as soon as day,
To fetch the summer home,
The summer and the radiant May,
For summer now is come.

In Madern vale the bell-flowers bloom,
And wave to Zephyr's breath:
The cuckoo sings in Morval Coombe,
Where nods the purple heath.

Come, dance around Glen-Aston tree—
We bring a garland gay,
And Mary of Guynear shall be
Our Lady of the May.

But where is William? Did he not declare,

He would be first the blossomed bough to bear!
She will not join the train! and see! the flower
She gathered now is fading! Hour by hour
She watched the sunshine on the thatch; again
Her mother turns the hour-glass; now, the pane
The westering sun has left—the long May-day
So Mary wore in hopes and fears away.
Slow twilight steals. By the small garden gate
She stands: Oh! William never came so late!
Her mother's voice is heard: Good child, come in;
Dream not of bliss on earth—it is a sin:
Come, take the Bible down, my child, and read;
In sickness, and in sorrow, and in need,
By friends forsaken, and by fears oppressed,
There only can the weary heart find rest.
Her thin hands, marked by many a wandering vein,
Her mother turned the silent glass again;
The rushlight now is lit, the Bible read,
Yet, ere sad Mary can retire to bed,
She listens!—Hark! no voice, no step she hears,—
Oh! seek thy bed to hide those bursting tears!
When the slow morning came, the tale was told,
(Need it have been?) that William's love was cold.
But hope yet whispers, dry the accusing tear,—
When Sunday comes, he will again be here!
And Sunday came, and struggling from a cloud.
The sun shone bright—the bells were chiming loud—
And lads and lasses, in their best attire,
Were tripping past—the youth, the child, the sire;
But William came not. With a boding heart
Poor Mary saw the Sunday crowd depart:
And when her mother came, with kerchief clean,
The last who tottered homeward o'er the green,
Mary, to hear no more of peace on earth,
Retired in silence to the lonely hearth.
Next day the tidings to the cottage came,
That William's heart confessed another flame:
That, with the bailiff's daughter he was seen,
At the new tabernacle on the green;
That cold and wayward falsehood made him prove
Alike a traitor to his faith and love.

The bells are ringing, it is Whitsuntide,—
And there goes faithless William with his bride.
Turn from the sight, poor Mary! Day by day,
The dread remembrance wore her heart away:
Untimely sorrow sat upon her cheek,
And her too trusting heart was left to break.

Six melancholy months have slowly passed,
And dark is heard November's hollow blast.
Sometimes, with tearful moodiness she smiled,
Then, still and placid looked, as when a child,
Or raised her eyes disconsolate and wild.
Oft, as she strayed the brook's green marge along,
She there would sing one sad and broken song:—

Lay me where the willows wave,
In the cold moonlight;
Shine upon my lowly grave,
Sadly, stars of night!

I to you would fly for rest,
But a stone, a stone,
Lies like lead upon my breast,
And every hope is flown.

Lay me where the willows wave,
In the cold moonlight;
Shine upon my lowly grave,
Sadly, stars of night!

Her mother said, Thou shalt not be confined,
Poor maid, for thou art harmless, and thy mind
The air may soothe, as fitfully it blows,
Whispering forgetfulness, if not repose.
So Mary wandered to the northern shore;
There oft she heard the gaunt Tregagel roar
Among the rocks; and when the tempest blew,
And, like the shivered foam, her long hair flew,
And all the billowy space was tossing wide,
Rock on! thou melancholy main, she cried,
I love thy voice, oh, ever-sounding sea,
Nor heed this sad world while I look on thee!
Then on the surge she gazed, with vacant stare,
Or tripping with wild fennel in her hair,
Sang merrily: Oh! we must dry the tear,
For Mab, the queen of fairies, will be here,—
William, she shall know all!—and then again
Her ditty died into its first sad strain:—

Lay me where the willows wave,
In the cold moonlight;
Shine upon my lowly grave,
Sadly, stars of night!

When home returned, the tears ran down apace;

She looked in silence in her mother's face;
Then, starting up, with wilder aspect cried,
How happy shall we be at Whitsuntide,
Then, mother, I shall be a bride—a bride!
Ah! some dire thought seems in her breast to rise,
Stern with terrific joy she rolls her eyes:
Her mother heeded not; nor when she took,
With more impatient haste, her Sunday book,
She heeded not—for age had dimmed her sight.
Her mother now is left alone: 'tis night.
Mary! poor Mary! her sad mother cried,
Mary! my Mary!—but no voice replied.

Next morn, light-hearted William passed along,
And careless hummed a desultory song,
Bound to St Ives' revel. Not a ray
Yet streaked the pale dawn of the dubious day;
The sun is yet below the hills: but, look!
There is the tower—the mill—the stile—the brook,—
And there is Mary's cottage! All is still!
Listen! no sound is heard but of the mill.
'Tis true, the toils of day are not begun,
But Mary always rose before the sun.
Still at the door, a leafless relic now,
Appeared a remnant of the May-day bough;
No hour-glass, in the window, tells the hours:
Where is poor Mary, where her book, her flowers?
Ah! was it fancy?—as he passed along,
He thought he heard a spirit's feeble song.
Struck by the thrilling sound, he turned his look.
Upon the ground there lay an open book;
One page was folded down:—Spirit of grace!
See! there are soils, like tear-blots, on the place!
It is a prayer-book! Soon these words he read;
Let him be desolate, and beg his bread!
Let there be none, not one, on earth to bless,—
Be his days few,—his children fatherless,—
His wife a widow!—let there be no friend
In his last moments mercy to extend!
It was a prayer-book he before had seen:
Where? when? Once more, wild terror on his mien,
He read the page:—An outcast let him lie,
And unlamented and forsaken die!
When he has children, may they pine away
Before his sight,—his wife to grief a prey.
Ah! 'tis poor Mary's book!—the very same
He read with her at church; and, lo! her name:—
The book of Mary Banks;—when this you see,

And I am dead and gone, remember me!
He trembles: mark!—the dew is on his brow:
The curse is hers! he cried—I feel it now!
I see already, even at my right hand,
Dead Mary, thy accusing spirit stand!
I feel thy deep, last curse! Then, with a cry,
He sunk upon the earth in agony.
Feebly he rose,—when, on the matted hair
Of a drowned maid, and on her bosom bare,
The sun shone out; how horrid, the first glance
Of sunlight, on that altered countenance!
The eyes were open, but though cold and dim,
Fixed with accusing ghastliness on him!
Merciful God! with faltering voice he cries,
Hide me! oh, hide me from the sight! Those eyes—
They glare on me! oh, hide me with the dead!
The curse, the deep curse rests upon my head!
Alas, poor maid! 'twas frenzy fired thy breast,
Which prompted horrors not to be expressed:
Whilst ever at thy side the foul fiend stood,
And, laughing, pointed to the oblivious flood.
William, heart-stricken, to despair a prey,
Soon left the village, journeying far away.
For, as if Mary's ghost in judgment cried,
His wife, in the first pains of child-birth, died.
Who has not heard, St Cuthbert, of thy well?
Perhaps the spirit may his fortunes tell.
He dropped a pebble—mark! no bubble bright
Comes from the bottom—turn away thy sight!
He looks again: O God! those eye-balls glare
How terribly! Ah, smooth that matted hair!
Mary! dear Mary! thy cold corse I see
Rise from the fountain! Look not thus at me!
I cannot bear the sight, that form, that look!
Oh! shut the book, dear Mary, shut the book!
Meantime, poor Mary in the grave was laid;—
Her lone and gray-haired mother wept and prayed:
Soon to the dust she followed; and, unknown,
There they both rest without a name or stone.
The village maids, who pass in summer by,
Still stop and say one prayer, for charity!
But what of William? Hide me in the mine!
He cried, the beams of day insulting shine!
Earth's very shadows are too gay, too bright,—
Hide me for ever in forgetful night!
In vain—that form, the cause of all his woes,
More sternly terrible in darkness rose!
Nearer he saw, with its pale waving hand,

The phantom in appalling stillness stand;
The letters of the book shone through the night,
More blasting! Hide, oh hide me from the sight!
Ocean, to thee and to thy storms I bring
A heart, that not the music of the spring,
Nor summer piping on the rural plain,
Shall ever wake to happiness again!
Ocean, be mine,—wild as thy wastes, to roam
From clime to clime!—Ocean, be thou my home!
Some say he died: here he was seen no more;
He went to sea; and oft, amid the roar
Of the wild waters, starting from his sleep,
He gazed upon the wild tempestuous deep;
When, slowly rising from the vessel's lee,
A shape appeared, which none besides could see;
Then would he shriek, like one whom Heaven forsook,
Oh! shut the book, dear Mary, shut the book!
In foreign lands, in darkness or in light,
The same dread spectre stood before his sight;
If slumber came his aching lids to close,
Funereal forms in long procession rose.
Sometimes he dreamed that every grief was past
Mary, long lost on earth, is found at last;
And now she smiled as when, in early life,
She lived in hope that she should be his wife;
The maids are dressed in white, and all are gay,
For this (he dreamed) is Mary's wedding-day!
Then wherefore sad? a chill comes o'er his soul,—
The sounds of mirth are hushed; and, hark! a toll!—
A slow, deep toll; and lo! a sable train
Of mourners, moving to the village fane.
A coffin now is laid in holy ground,
That, heavily, returns a hollow sound,
When the first earth upon its lid is thrown:
That hollow sound now changes to a groan:
While, rising with wan cheek, and dripping hair,
And moving lips, and eyes of ghastly glare,
The spectre comes again! It comes more near!
'Tis Mary! and that book with many a tear
Is wet, which, with dim fingers, long and cold,
He sees her to the glimmering moon unfold.
And now her hand is laid upon his heart.
Gasping, he wakes—with a convulsive start,
He gazes round! Moonlight is on the tide—
The passing keel is scarcely heard to glide,—
See where the spectre goes! with frenzied look
He shrieks again, Oh! Mary, shut the book!
Now, to the ocean's verge the phantom flies,—

And, hark! far off, the lessening laughter dies.
Years passed away,—at night, or evening close,
Faint, and more faint, the accusing spectre rose.
Restored from toil and perils of the main,
Now William treads his native place again.
Near the Land's-end, upon the rudest shore,
Where, from the west, Atlantic surges roar,
He lived, a lonely stranger, sad, but mild;
All marked his sadness, chiefly when he smiled;
Some competence he gained, by years of toil:
So, in a cottage, on his native soil,
He dwelt, remote from crowds, nor told his tale
To human ear: he saw the white clouds sail
Oft o'er the bay, when suns of summer shone,
Yet still he wandered, muttering and alone.
At night, when, like the tumult of the tide,
Sinking to sad repose, all trouble died,
The book of God was on his pillow laid,
He wept upon it, and in secret prayed.
He had no friend on earth, save one blue jay,
Which, from the Mississippi, far away,
O'er the Atlantic, to his native land
He brought;—and this poor bird fed from his hand.
In the great world there was not one beside
For whom he cared, since his own mother died.
Yet manly strength was his, for twenty-years
Weighed light upon his frame, though passed in tears;
His age not forty-two, and in his face
Of care more than of age appeared the trace.
Mary was scarce remembered; by degrees,
The sights and sounds of life began to please.
Ruth was a widow, who, in youth, had known
Griefs of the heart, and losses of her own.
She, patient, mild, compassionate, and kind,
First woke to human sympathies his mind.
He looked affectionately, when her child
Caressed his bird, and then he stood and smiled.
This widow and her child, almost unknown,
Lived in a cottage that adjoined his own.
Her husband was a fisher, one whose life
Is fraught with terror to an anxious wife:
Night after night exposed upon the main;
Returning, tired with toil, or drenched with rain;
His gains, uncertain as his life; he knows
No stated hours of labour and repose.
When others to a cheerful home retire,
And his wife sits before the evening fire,
He, rocking in the dark, tempestuous night,

Haply is thinking of that social light.
Ruth's husband left the bay, the wind and rain
Came down, the tempest swept the howling main;
The boat sank in the storm, and he was found,
Below the rocks of the dark Lizard, drowned.
Seven years had passed, and after evening prayer,
To William's cottage Ruth would oft repair,
And with her little son would sometimes stay,
Listening to tales of regions far away.
The wondering boy loved of those scenes to hear—
Of battles—of the roving buccaneer—
Of the wild hunters, in the forest-glen,
And fires, and dances of the savage men.
So William spoke of perils he had passed,—
Of voices heard amid the roaring blast;
Of those who, lonely and of hope bereft,
Upon some melancholy rock are left,
Who mark, despairing, at the close of day,
Perhaps, some far-off vessel sail away.
He spoke with pity of the land of slaves—
And of the phantom-ship that rides the waves.
It comes! it comes! A melancholy light
Gleams from the prow upon the storm of night.
'Tis here! 'tis there! In vain the billows roll;
It steers right on, but not a living soul
Is there to guide its voyage through the dark,
Or spread the sails of that mysterious bark!
He spoke of vast sea-serpents, how they float
For many a rood, or near some hurrying boat
Lift up their tall neck, with a hissing sound,
And questing turn their bloodshot eye-balls round.
He spoke of sea-maids, on the desert rocks,
Who in the sun comb their green dripping locks,
While, heard at distance, in the parting ray,
Beyond the furthest promontory's bay,
Aërial music swells and dies away!
One night they longer stayed the tale to hear,
And Ruth that night "beguiled him of a tear,
Whene'er he told of the distressful stroke
Which his youth suffered." Then, she pitying spoke;
And from that night a softer feeling grew,
As calmer prospects rose within his view.
And why not, ere the long night of the dead,
The slow descent of life together tread?
The day is fixed; William no more shall roam,
William and Ruth shall have one heart—one home:
The world shut out, both shall together pray:
Both wait the evening of life's changeful day:

She shall his anguish soothe, when he is wild,
And he shall be a father to her child.
Fair rose the morn—the summer air how bland!
The blue wave scarcely seems to touch the land.
Again 'tis William's wedding-day! advance—
For lo! the church and blue slate of Penzance!
Their faith and troth is pledged, the rites are o'er,
The nuptial band winds slow along the shore,
The smiling boy beside. As thus they passed,
With sudden blackness rushed the impetuous blast;
Deep thunder rolled in long portentous sound,
At distance: nearer now, it shakes the ground.
Pale, William sinks, with speechless dread oppressed,
As the forked flash seems darted at his breast.
His beating heart is heard,—blanched is his cheek,—
A well-known voice seemed in the storm to speak;
Aghast he cried again, with frantic look,
Oh! shut the book, dear Mary, shut the book!
By late remorse he died; for, from that day,
The judgment on his head, he pined away,
And soon an outcast suicide he lay.
By the church-porch rests Mary of Guynear;—
When the first cuckoo startles the cold year,
And blue mint on her grave more beauteous grows,
One small bird seems to sing for her repose.
Near the Land's-end, so black and weather-beat,
He lies, and the dark sea is at his feet.
Thou, who hast heard the tale of the sad maid,
Know, conscious guilt is the accusing shade:
If thou hast loved some gentle maid and true,
Whose first affections never swerved from you;
Leave her not—oh! for pity and for truth,
Leave her not, tearful in her days of youth!
Too late, the pang of vain remorse shall start,
And Conscience thus avenge—a broken heart!

PART FOURTH

WALK ABROAD—VIEWS AROUND, FROM THE SEVERN TO BRISTOL—WRINGTON—"AULD ROBIN GRAY"

The shower is past—the heath-bell, at our feet,
Looks up, as with a smile, though the cold dew
Hangs yet within its cup, like Pity's tear
Upon the eyelids of a village child!
Mark! where a light upon those far-off waves

Gleams, while the passing shower above our head
Sheds its last silent drops, amid the hues
Of the fast-fading rainbow,—such is life!
Let us go forth, the redbreast is abroad,
And, dripping in the sunshine, sings again.
No object on the wider sea-line meets
The straining vision, but one distant ship,
Hanging, as motionless and still, far off,
In the pale haze, between the sea and sky.
She seems the ship—the very ship I saw
In infancy, and in that very place,
Whilst I, and all around me, have grown old
Since she was first descried; and there she sits,
A solitary thing of the wide main—
As she sat years ago. Yet she moves on:—
To-morrow all may be one waste of waves!
Where is she bound? We know not; and no voice
Will tell us where. Perhaps she beats her way
Slow up the channel, after many years,
Returning from some distant clime, or lands,
Beyond the Atlantic! Oh! what anxious eyes
Count every nearer surge that heaves around!
How many anxious hearts this moment beat
With thronging thoughts of home, till those fixed eyes,
Intensely fixed upon these very hills,
Are filled with tears! Perhaps she wanders on—
On—on—into the world of the vast sea,
There to be lost: never, with homeward sails,
Destined to greet these far-seen hills again,
Now fading into mist! So let her speed,
And we will pray she may return in joy,
When every storm is past! Such is this sea,
That shows one wandering ship! How different smile
The sea-scenes of the south; and chiefly thine,
Waters of loveliest Hampton, chiefly thine—
Where I have passed the happiest hours of youth—
Waters of loveliest Hampton! Thy gray walls,
And loop-hooled battlements, cast the same shade
Upon the light blue wave, as when of yore,
Beneath their arch, King Canute sat, and chid
The tide, that came regardless to his feet,
A thousand years ago. Oh! how unlike
Yon solitary sea, the summer shines,
There, while a crowd of glancing vessels glide,
Filled with the young and gay, and pennants wave,
And sails, at distance, beautifully swell
To the light breeze, or pass, like butterflies,
Amid the smoking steamers. And, oh look!—

Look! what a fairy lady is that yacht
That turns the wooded point, and silently
Streams up the sylvan Itchin; silently—
And yet as if she said, as she went on,
Who does not gaze at me!
Yon winding sands
Were solitary once, as the wide sea.
Such I remember them! No sound was heard,
Save of the sea-gull warping on the wind,
Or of the surge that broke along the shore,
Sad as the seas; and can I e'er forget,
When, once, a visitor from Oxenford,
Proud of Wintonian scholarship, a youth,
Silent, but yet light-hearted, deeming here
I could have no companion fit for him—
So whispered youthful vanity—for him
Whom Oxford had distinguished,—can my heart
Forget when once, with thoughts like these, at morn,
I wandered forth alone! The first ray shone
On the white sea-gull's wing, and gazing round,
I listened to the tide's advancing roar,
When, for the old and booted fisherman,
Who silent dredged for shrimps, in the cold haze
Of sunrise, I beheld—or was it not
A momentary vision?—a fair form—
A female, following, with light, airy step,
The wave as it retreated, and again
Tripping before it, till it touched her foot,
As if in play; and she stood beautiful,
Like to a fairy sea-maid of the deep,
Graceful, and young, and on the sands alone.
I looked that she would vanish! She had left,
Like me, just left the abode of discipline,
And came, in the gay fulness of her heart,
When the pale light first glanced along the wave,
To play with the wild ocean, like a child;
And though I knew her not, I vowed (oh, hear,
Ye votaries of German sentiment!)—
Vowed an eternal love; but, diffident,
I cast a parting look, that seemed to say,
Shall we ne'er meet again? The vision smiled,
And left the scene to solitude. Once more
We met, and then we parted, in this world
To meet no more; and that fair form, that shone
The vision of a moment, on the sands,
Was never seen again! Now it has passed
Where all things are forgotten; but it shone
To me a sparkle of the morning sun,

That trembled on the light wave yesterday,
And perished there for ever!
Look around!
Above the winding reach of Severn stands,
With massy fragments of forsaken towers,
Thy castle, solitary Walton. Hark!
Through the lone ivied arch, was it the wind
Came fitful! There, by moonlight, we might stand,
And deem it some old castle of romance;
And on the glimmering ledge of yonder rock,
Above the wave, fancy it was the form
Of a spectre-lady, for a moment seen,
Lifting her bloody dagger, then with shrieks
Vanishing! Hush! there is no sound—no sound
But of the Severn sweeping onward! Look!
There is no bleeding apparition there—
No fiery phantoms glare along thy walls!
Surrounded by the works of silent art,
And far, far more endearing, by a group
Of breathing children, their possessor lives;
And ill should I deserve the name of bard—
Of courtly bard, if I could touch this theme
Without a prayer—an earnest, heartfelt prayer,
When one, whose smile I never saw but once,
Yet cannot well forget, when one now blooms—
Unlike the spectre-lady of the rock—
A living and a lovely bride!
How proud,
Opposed to Walton's silent towers, how proud,
With all her spires and fanes, and volumed smoke,
Trailing in columns to the midday sun,
Black, or pale blue, above the cloudy haze,
And the great stir of commerce, and the noise
Of passing and repassing wains, and cars,
And sledges, grating in their underpath,
And trade's deep murmur, and a street of masts
And pennants from all nations of the earth,
Streaming below the houses, piled aloft,
Hill above hill; and every road below
Gloomy with troops of coal-nymphs, seated high
On their rough pads, in dingy dust serene:—
How proudly, amid sights and sounds like these,
Bristol, through all whose smoke, dark and aloof,
Stands Redcliff's solemn fane,—how proudly girt
With villages, and Clifton's airy rocks,
Bristol, the mistress of the Severn sea—
Bristol, amid her merchant-palaces,
That ancient city sits!

From out those trees,
Look! Congresbury lifts its slender spire!
How many woody glens and nooks of shade,
With transient sunshine, fill the interval,
As rich as Poussin's landscapes! Gnarled oaks,
Dark, or with fits of desultory light
Flung through the branches, there o'erhang the road,
Where sheltered, as romantic, Brockley-Coombe
Allures the lingering traveller to wind,
Step by step, up its sylvan hollow, slow,
Till, the proud summit gained, how gloriously
The wide scene lies in light! how gloriously
Sun, shadows, and blue mountains far away,
Woods, meadows, and the mighty Severn blend,
While the gray heron up shoots, and screams for joy!
There the dark yew starts from the limestone rock
Into faint sunshine; there the ivy hangs
From the old oak, whose upper branches, bare,
Seem as admonishing the nether woods
Of Time's swift pace; while dark and deep beneath
The fearful hollow yawns, upon whose edge
One peeping cot sends up, from out the fern,
Its early wreath of slow-ascending smoke.
And who lives in that far-secluded cot?
Poor Dinah! She was once a serving-maid,
Most beautiful; now, on the wild wood's edge
She lives alone, alone, and bowed with age,
Muttering, and sad, and scarce within the sound
Of human kind, forsaken as the scene!
Nor pass we Fayland, with its fairy rings
Marking the turf, where tiny elves may dance,
Their light feet twinkling in the dewy gleam,
By moonlight. But what sullen demon piled
The rocks, that stern in desolation frown,
Through the deep solitude of Goblin-Coombe,
Where, wheeling o'er its crags, the shrilling kite
More dismal makes its utter dreariness!
But yonder, at the foot of Mendip, smiles
The seat of cultivated Addington:
And there, that beautiful but solemn church
Presides o'er the still scene, where one old friend
Lives social, while the shortening day unfelt
Steals on, and eve, with smiling light, descends—
With smiling light, that, lingering on the tower,
Reminds earth's pilgrim of his lasting home.
Is that a magic garden on the edge
Of Mendip hung? Even so it seems to gleam;
While many a cottage, on to Wrington's smoke

(Wrington, the birth-place of immortal Locke),
Chequers the village-crofts and lowly glens
With porch of flowers, and bird-cage, at the door,
That seems to say—England, with all thy crimes,
And smitten as thou art by pauper-laws,
England, thou only art the poor man's home!
And yonder Blagdon, in its sheltered glen,
Sits pensive, like a rock-bird in its cleft.
The craggy glen here winds, with ivy hung,
Beneath whose dark, depending tresses peeps
The Cheddar-pink; there fragments of red rock
Start from the verdant turf, among the flowers.
And who can paint sweet Blagdon, and not think
Of Langhorne, in that hermitage of song—
Langhorne, a pastor, and a poet too!
He, in retirement's literary bower,
Oft wooed the Sisters of the sacred well,
Harmonious: nor pass on without a prayer
For her, associate of his early fame,
Accomplished, eloquent, and pious More,
Who now, with slow and gentle decadence,
In the same vale, with look upraised to heaven,
Waits meekly at the gate of paradise,
Smiling at time!
But, hark! there comes a song,
Of Scotland's lakes and hills—Auld Robin Gray!
Tweed, or the winding Tay, ne'er echoed words
More sadly soothing; but the melody,
Like some sweet melody of olden times,
A ditty of past days, rose from those woods.
Oh! could I hear it, as I heard it once—
Sung by a maiden of the south, whose look
(Although her song be sweet), whose look, and life,
Are sweeter than her song—no minstrel gray,
Like Donald and "the Lady of the Lake,"
But would lay down his harp, and when the song
Was ended, raise his lighted eyes, and smile,
To thank that maiden, with a strain like this:—

Oh! when I hear thee sing of "Jamie far away,"
Of "father and of mother," and of "Auld Robin Gray,"
I listen till I think it is Jeanie's self I hear,
And I look in thy face with a blessing and a tear.

"I look in thy face," for my heart it is not cold,
Though winter's frost is stealing on, and I am growing old;
Those tones I shall remember as long as I live,
And a blessing and a tear shall be the thanks I give.

The tear it is for summers that so blithesome have been,
For the flowers that all are faded, and the days that I have seen;
The blessing, lassie, is for thee, whose song, so sadly sweet,
Recalls the music of "Lang Syne," to which my heart has beat.

PART FIFTH

LANG SYNE—VISION OF THE DELUGE—CONCLUSION

The music of "Lang Syne!" Oh! long ago
It died away—died, and was heard no more!
And where those hills that skirt the level vale,
On to the left, the prospect intercept,
I would not, could not look, were they removed;
I would not, could not look, lest I should see
The sunshine on that spot of all the world,
Where, starting from the dream of youth, I gazed
Long since, on the cold, clouded world, and cried,
Beautiful vision, loved, adored, in vain,
Farewell—farewell, for ever!
How sincere,
How pure was my heart's love! oh! was it not?
Yes; Heaven can witness, now my brow is changed,
And I look back, and almost seem to hear
The music of the days when we were young,
Like music in a dream, ere we awoke,
Oh! witness, Heaven, how fervent, how sincere—
How fervent, and how tender, and how pure,
Was my fond heart's first love!
The summer eve
Shone, as with sympathy of sweet farewell,
Upon thy Tor, and solitary mound,
Glaston, as rapidly I passed along,
Borne from those scenes for ever, while with song
The sorrows of the hour and way beguiled.
So passed the days of youth, which ne'er return,
Tearful; for worldly fortune smiled too late,
And the poor minstrel-boy had then no wealth,
Save such as poets dream of—love and hope.
At Fortune's frown, the wreath which Hope entwined
Lay withering, for the dream had been too sweet
For human life; yet never, though his love,
All his fond love, he muttered to the winds;
Though oft he strove, distempered, without joy,
To drown even the remembrance that he lived—

Never a weak complaint escaped his lip,
Save that some tender tones, as he passed on,
Died on his desultory lyre.
No more!
Forget the shadows of a feverish dream,
That long has passed away! Uplift the eyes
To Him who sits above the water flood,—
To Him who was, and is, and is to come!
Wrapped in the view of ages that are passed,
And marking here the record of earth's doom,
Let us, even now, think that we hear the sound—
The sound of the great flood, the peopled earth
Covering and surging in its solitude!
Let us forget the passing hour, the stir
Of this tumultuous scene of human things,
And bid imagination lift the veil
Spread o'er the rolling globe four thousand years!
The vision of the deluge! Hark—a trump!
It was the trump of the Archangel! Stern
He stands, whilst the awakening thunder rolls
Beneath his feet! Stern, and alone, he stands
Upon Imaus' height!
No voice is heard
Of revelry or blasphemy so high!
He sounds again his trumpet; and the clouds
Come deepening o'er the world!
Why art thou pale?
A strange and fearful stillness is on earth,
As if the shadow of the Almighty passed
O'er the abodes of man, and hushed at once
The song, the shout, the cries of violence,
The groan of the oppressed, and the deep curse
Of blasphemy, that scowls upon the clouds,
And mocks the deeper thunder!
Hark! a voice—
Perish! Again the thunder rolls; the earth
Answers, from north to south, from east to west—
Perish! The fountains of the mighty deep
Are broken up; the rushing rains descend,
Like night—deep night; while, momentary seen,
Through blacker clouds, on his pale phantom-horse,
Death, a gigantic skeleton, rides on,
Rejoicing, where the millions of mankind—
Visible, where his lightning-arrows glared—
Welter beneath the shadow of his horse!
Now, dismally, through all her caverns, Hell
Sends forth a horrid laugh, that dies away,
And then a loud voice answers—Victory!

Victory to the rider and his horse!
Victory to the rider and his horse!
Ride on:—the ark, majestic and alone
On the wide waste of the careering deep,
Its hull scarce peering through the night of clouds,
Is seen. But, lo! the mighty deep has shrunk!
The ark, from its terrific voyage, rests
On Ararat. The raven is sent forth,—
Send out the dove, and as her wings far off
Shine in the light, that streaks the severing clouds,
Bid her speed on, and greet her with a song:—

Go, beautiful and gentle dove;
But whither wilt thou go?
For though the clouds ride high above,
How sad and waste is all below!

The wife of Shem, a moment to her breast
Held the poor bird, and kissed it. Many a night
When she was listening to the hollow wind,
She pressed it to her bosom, with a tear;
Or when it murmured in her hand, forgot
The long, loud tumult of the storm without.
She kisses it, and at her father's word,
Bids it go forth.

The dove flies on! In lonely flight
She flies from dawn till dark;
And now, amid the gloom of night,
Comes weary to the ark.
Oh! let me in, she seems to say,
For long and lone hath been my way!
Oh! once more, gentle mistress, let me rest,
And dry my dripping plumage on thy breast!

So the bird flew to her who cherished it.
She sent it forth again out of the ark;—
Again it came at evening fall, and, lo!
An olive-leaf plucked off, and in its bill.
And Shem's wife took the green leaf from its bill,
And kissed its wings again, and smilingly
Dropped on its neck one silent tear for joy.
She sent it forth once more; and watched its flight,
Till it was lost amid the clouds of heaven:
Then gazing on the clouds where it was lost,
Its mournful mistress sung this last farewell:—

Go, beautiful and gentle dove,

And greet the morning ray;
For, lo! the sun shines bright above,
And night and storm have passed away.
No longer, drooping, here confined,
In this cold prison dwell;
Go, free to sunshine and to wind,
Sweet bird, go forth, and fare thee well!

Oh! beautiful and gentle dove,
Thy welcome sad will be,
When thou shalt hear no voice of love,
In murmurs from the leafy tree:
Yet freedom, freedom shalt thou find,
From this cold prison's cell;
Go, then, to sunshine and the wind,
Sweet bird, go forth, and fare thee well!

And never more she saw it; for the earth
Was dry, and now, upon the mountain's van,
Again the great Archangel stands; the light
Of the moist rainbow glitters on his hair—
He to the bow uplifts his hands, whose arch
Spans the whole heaven; and whilst, far off, in light,
The ascending dove is for a moment seen,
The last rain falls—falls, gently and unheard.
Amid the silent sunshine! Oh! look up!—
Above the clouds, borne up the depth of light,
Behold a cross!—and round about the cross,
Lo! angels and archangels jubilant,
Till the ascending pomp in light is lost,
Lift their acclaiming voice—Glory to thee,
Glory, and praise, and honour be to thee,
Lord God of hosts; we laud and magnify
Thy glorious name, praising Thee evermore,
For the great dragon is cast down, and hell
Vanquished beneath thy cross, Lord Jesus Christ!
Hark! the clock strikes! The shadowy scene dissolves,
And all the visionary pomp is past!
I only see a few sheep on the edge
Of this aërial ridge, and Banwell Tower,
Gray in the morning sunshine, at our feet.
Farewell to Banwell Cave, and Banwell Hill,
And Banwell Church; and farewell to the shores
Where, when a child, I wandered; and farewell,
Harp of my youth! Above this mountain-cave
I leave thee, murmuring to the fitful breeze
That wanders from that sea, whose sound I heard
So many years ago.

Yet, whilst the light
Steals from the clouds, to rest upon that tower,
I turn a parting look, and lift to Heaven
A parting prayer, that our own Zion, thus,—
With sober splendour, yet not gorgeous,
Her mitred brow tempered with lenity
And apostolic mildness—in her mien
No dark defeature, beautiful as mild,
And gentle as the smile of charity,—
Thus on the Rock of Ages may uplift
Her brow majestic, pointing to the spires
That grace her village glens, or solemn fanes
In cities, calm above the stir and smoke,
And listening to deep harmonies that swell
From all her temples!
So may she adorn—
Her robe as graceful, as her creed is pure—
This happy land, till time shall be no more!
And whilst her gray cathedrals rise in air,
Solemn, august, and beautiful, and touched
By time, to show a grace, but no decay,
Like that fair pile, which, from hoar Mendip's brow,
The traveller beholds, crowning the vale
Of Avalon, with all its towers in light;
So, England, may thy gray cathedrals lift
Their front in heaven's pure light, and ever boast
Such prelate-lords—bland, but yet dignified—
Pious, paternal, and beloved, as he
Who prompted, and forgives, this Severn song!
And thou, O Lord and Saviour! on whose rock
That Church is founded, though the storm without
May howl around its battlements, preserve
Its spirit, and still pour into the hearts
Of all, who there confess thy holy name,
Peace, that, through evil or through good report,
They may hold on their blameless way!
For me,
Though disappointment, like a morning cloud,
Hung on my early hopes, that cloud is passed,—
Is passed, but not forgotten,—and the light
Is calm, not cold, which rests upon the scene,
Soon to be ended. I may wake no more
The melody of song on earth; but Thee,
Father of Heaven, and Saviour, at this hour,
Father and Lord, I thank Thee that no song
Of mine, from youth to age, has left a stain
I would blot out; and grateful for the good
Thy providence, through many years, has lent,

Humbly I wait the close, till Thy high will
Dismiss me,—blessed if, when that hour shall come,
My life may plead, far better than my song.

William Lisle Bowles – A Short Biography

William Lisle Bowles was born on 24th September 1762 at King's Sutton in Northamptonshire.

His great-grandfather, grandfather and his father, William Thomas Bowles, had all been parish priests and inevitably Bowles would join their line.

At the age of 14 he entered Winchester College, where the headmaster was Dr Joseph Warton (a minor poet, his most notable piece is The Enthusiast, 1744. In 1755, he taught at Winchester and from 1766 to 1793 was headmaster. His career as a critic was illustrious. He produced editions of poets such as Virgil as well as several English poets).

In 1789 Bowles published, a small quarto volume, Fourteen Sonnets, which was received with extraordinary praise, not only by the general public, but by such revered poets as Samuel Taylor Coleridge and Wordsworth.

The Sonnets were a return to an older and purer poetic style, and by their grace of expression, lyrical versification, tender tone of feeling and vivid appreciation of the wonder and beauty of nature, stood out in marked contrast to the elaborate works which then formed the bulk of English poetry.

Bowles said "Poetic trifles from solitary rambles whilst chewing the cud of sweet and bitter fancy, written from memory, confined to fourteen lines, this seemed best adapted to the unity of sentiment, the verse flowed in unpremeditated harmony as my ear directed but are far from being mere elegiac couplets".

The young Samuel Taylor Coleridge felt obliged to record his debt of gratitude to Bowles: "My obligations to Mr. Bowles were indeed important, and for radical good. At a very premature age, ... I had bewildered myself in metaphysicks, and in theological controversy. Nothing else pleased me. Poetry ... became insipid to me.... This preposterous pursuit was, beyond doubt, injurious both to my natural powers, and to the progress of my education.... But from this I was auspiciously withdrawn, chiefly by the genial influence of a style of poetry, so tender and yet so manly, so natural and real, and yet so dignified and harmonious, as the sonnets &c. of Mr. Bowles!"

In 1781 Bowles left as captain of Winchester school, and proceeded to Trinity College, Oxford, after winning a scholarship. Two years later he won the Chancellor's prize for Latin verse. It was now evident that the Church and poetry were to be his two callings.

After receiving his degree at Oxford, Bowles now began his career in service to the Church of England. In 1792, after serving as curate in Donhead St Andrew, Bowles was appointed vicar of Chicklade in Wiltshire.

Five years later, in 1797, he received the vicarage of Dumbleton in Gloucestershire, and in 1804 became vicar of Bremhill in Wiltshire, where he wrote the poem seen on Maud Heath's statue. In the same year his bishop, John Douglas, collated him to a prebendal stall in Salisbury Cathedral.

In 1818 Bowles was made chaplain to the Prince Regent, and in 1828 he was elected residentiary canon of Salisbury.

His years of service perhaps diminished both his stature as a poet and certainly the way he was viewed. For much of his career Bowles was seen as rather soft when set against his contemporaries but in the end his ability as a poet was enshrined, after a long and ferocious attack against him, by the principles he so eloquently wrote about and adhered too.

It is as well to remember that when critics suggest that compared to other poets his longer works were not to the standard that the competition achieved, that this era is perhaps without poetic equal. Set against Byron, Shelley, Keats, Wordsworth and other great luminaries of the era it is perhaps difficult to see his works in isolation for their own value.

The longer poems published by Bowles are distinguished by purity of imagination, cultured and graceful diction, and a great thoughtfulness of feeling. Among them were The Spirit of Discovery (1804), which alas was so mercilessly ridiculed by Byron; The Missionary (1813); The Grave of the Last Saxon (1822); and St John in Patmos (1833).

In 1806 he published an edition of Alexander Pope's works with notes and an essay, in which he laid down certain canons as to poetic imagery which, subject to some modification, were later accepted, but received at the time with strong opposition by admirers of Pope.

Bowles restated his views in 1819, in The Invariable Principles of Poetry. The controversy brought into sharp contrast the opposing views of poetry, which may be thought of as being either the natural or the artificial.

In personality and nature Bowles was said to be an amiable, absent-minded, but rather eccentric man. His poems speak warmly of a refinement of feeling, tenderness, and pensive thought, but are lacking in power and passion. But that should not diminish their value or appreciation to us.

Bowles maintained that images drawn from nature are poetically finer than those drawn from art; and that in the highest kinds of poetry the themes or passions handled should be of the general or elemental kind, and not the transient manners of any society. These positions were attacked by Byron, Thomas Campbell, William Roscoe and others, and for a time Bowles had to fight his corner on his own. Soon however, William Hazlitt and the Blackwood critics came to his assistance, and on the whole Bowles had reason to congratulate himself on having established certain principles which might serve as the basis of a true method of poetical criticism, and of having inaugurated, both by precept and by example, a new era in English poetry.

As well as his poetry Bowles was also responsible for writing a Life of Bishop Ken (in two volumes, 1830–1831), Coombe Ellen and St. Michael's Mount (1798), The Battle of the Nile (1799), and The Sorrows of Switzerland (1801).

Bowles also enjoyed considerable reputation as an antiquary and his principal work in that field was Hermes Britannicus (1828).

William Lisle Bowles died on April 7th, 1850 at the age of 87.

www.ingramcontent.com/pod-product-compliance
Lightning Source LLC
Chambersburg PA
CBHW060056050426
42448CB00011B/2490